SHOOTING GAME

Michael Kemp

❦ ❦ ❦

Shooting Game

Adam & Charles Black
London

FIRST PUBLISHED 1972
A. & C. BLACK LTD
4, 5 & 6 SOHO SQUARE LONDON W1V 6AD

© 1972 MICHAEL KEMP

ISBN: 0 7136 1338 6

PRINTED IN GREAT BRITAIN BY
CLARKE, DOBLE & BRENDON LTD
PLYMOUTH

Contents

Photographs

*With the exception of those facing pages 144 and 145, all the photo-
graphs for this book were specially taken by John Marchington Esq.*

Figures

Introduction

It used to be fashionable to say airily that nothing worth knowing could be learned from a book, but if it were ever true the time has gone. Tommy Armour's great book *How to Play Your Best Golf All The Time* must have gone far towards destroying the belief and John Hislop's *Steeplechasing* cannot be read without imparting knowledge to the reader. On a lower plane I learned to bowl both a googly and a top-spinner from a book and many of us have learned to re-decorate our houses in the same way.

It is true that your shooting would not benefit if you read right through this book, bought a gun and then tried to follow my instructions. But if you read with a gun by your side, constantly putting the book down and trying to manipulate the gun in the manner described, you will learn a great deal. Things would be ideal if, after you had read and practised one chapter, we could go to the shooting ground together. When I was certain that you had mastered one lesson you would be introduced to the next; then you would go home, read the book, practice by yourself and return when the second lesson had been digested.

We cannot shoot together but you may be able to follow the same routine at some shooting school. That may be the best course available but do not despair if no school is within reach, for you will be able to devise something which will serve your purpose.

Because the reader should study the text for a few minutes and then handle his gun for a time the chapters in the part of the book devoted to handling a gun have been kept very short. Also, although women can shoot every bit as well as men, the book has been written as though every reader were a man who shot from his right shoulder. I ask ladies to be understanding and left-handers to make their own adjustments.

Safety

So much has already been written about the imperative need for handling guns safely at all times that I do not wish to add to it—it is assumed that the reader has already learned all that print can teach on this subject and that every novice will be supervised until the proper handling of a gun has become second nature.

In *Gun Safety* Roderick Willett devotes a whole book to the subject. It is published by Arlington Books. Churchill's *Game Shooting* has a chapter on the elements of gun-handling and many cautions and instructions throughout the text. There is also a section on the safe handling of guns in *Rough Shooting* by Gurney A. Grattan and Roderick Willett, published by Faber & Faber, and many, if not most, shooting anthologies contain Commander Mark Beaufoy's poem which is always referred to as 'Never, never let your gun', but whose proper name is 'A Father's Advice To His Son'. *Gun Code* gives essential advice on handling a gun, and is published by the British Field Sports Society (address on page 113).

Much of the material contained in this book has already appeared in *Shooting Times & Country Magazine*, although I have taken the opportunity presented by publication in its present form to re-write and to expand the original articles.

I am very grateful to the Editor not only for permission to make use of the material in this manner but for the help and encouragement he has always given to me, and I am glad to have this opportunity of thanking him most warmly.

Part One
Learning to Shoot

1

The Modern Approach

When a keen novice is first introduced to a shotgun he usually spends as much time as possible with the gun in his hands and reads all the available literature connected with shooting. He finds that there is a wealth of writing about game and guns but very little about the skilful handling of the gun itself. This is a great pity because shooting with a shotgun, like riding a horse, is something which can be picked up but is done very much better after proper teaching from the outset.

Within my own lifetime the average standard of riding has improved enormously because the Pony Club has spread the realization that riding must be studied, but I suspect that the general standard of shooting has fallen because the idea that it is something which a real man can do well by instinct has lingered on while the opportunities for practice have diminished. Such an idea was never well founded. The remarkable improvement which even a few lessons make to the performance of men who have been below average for decades supports this opinion and the few men I know who shoot well, although they had no formal instruction, all spent their childhood in a shooting atmosphere where they probably picked up sound methods unconsciously.

The initial teaching I received was crystallized in a book by Charles Lancaster containing many pictures showing the point ahead of the bird at which the gun should be aimed for a vast variety of shots. It was an old book even then but it was arguably the best instructional work published before Churchill's *Game Shooting*. It teaches a method which I call 'Forward Allowance', and which will be examined in detail later. Our ancestors were compelled to adopt some such system because there was an uncertain and variable interval of time between the pressing of the trigger and the discharge of the gun. It is mathematically sound, and if only the necessary data could be gathered, the calculations made and the gun directed in the time available, wonderful results would be obtained. In practice it is of limited value to the game shot but it is not without merit: generations of shooting men have used it but no-one can reach his full potential by its use alone.

Robert Churchill's book *Game Shooting* was first published in 1955 by Michael Joseph Ltd, and it sets out an entirely different method. The essence of his system is, broadly, that the shooter should focus his eyes upon the moving bird; when properly mounted a correctly-fitted gun will then always point at the bird until the man swings it ahead 'subconsciously' and fires at the right instant. Now the words of the author of *Game Shooting* carry great weight, for he was also the Churchill of the XXV gun, a renowned ballistics expert and innovator, an outstanding game shot and a famous teacher of shooting. In his own sphere he stands very high indeed and it is not my purpose to denigrate this great man for whom, and for whose method of shooting, I have the greatest admiration. Beyond question it is an excellent method once a trained man has a well-fitted gun.

One of my purposes is to enable aspirants to take that most difficult step, from the realization that some allowance must be made to the bottom rung of Churchill's ladder. Once the novice is safely on that rung practice will carry him to the highest level his natural talent permits, but reaching the foot of the ladder is far from easy: the beginner has neither a gun which fits, an eye which makes correct allowances subconsciously, nor trained muscles which execute the brain's orders. He must learn to shoot in stages. First he must develop a co-ordination of eye, movement and balance together with a consistent style. Then he must obtain a gun which really fits him and, if he makes the slight variation in technique which is the only significant difference between the method I advocate and Churchill's, he will be securely on the ladder. But not everyone wishes to change to the Churchill swing.

The Smoke Trail method, which I advocate, is no new thing and experience has shown that most beginners find it easier to learn than any other. Some, having mastered it, change to the Churchill method but many remain smoke trailers for life and there is a reason for this. Churchill's method is very far from the middle of the road and, like his XXV gun, it does not suit everybody. For some it is the epitome of excellence, but others find it exaggerated; they get better results by going most of the way with Churchill but staying a trifle nearer the centre of the road.

It is certainly true that no one method is best suited to every shooting man, and self-evident that if the target is consistently struck by the centre of the pattern no theorist should cavil, but it is important that every beginner should acquire a sound technique upon which he can fall back when things go wrong. I distrust shooting by flair alone for there is no second line of defence in times of trouble; flair men are often brilliant when all is going well but they plumb the depths when Lady Luck frowns. A man who has been properly taught and has developed a sound technique loses brilliance when he strikes a bad patch, but he remains a sound workman at all times.

Many pupils ask why they cannot start with a properly fitted gun and the answer is that they can, and should, start with one that is a reasonable fit—the stock will be about the right length and the bend and cast-off more or less correct. It might be a perfect fit as a ready-made suit might be, by blind chance, but that is all. The probability is that some alterations will be necessary later, for the cleverest maker in the world cannot tailor a stock to fit a man who puts the butt onto a different part of his shoulder three times out of five and does not even hold his gun in precisely the same way for three consecutive shots. But once the shooter has developed a consistent style the maker can fashion a stock which fits as well as a suit from Savile Row. Such a gun opens an entirely new vista; it removes all the toil and is as great an aid to shooting as a slide rule is to arithmetic.

Diagrams illustrating different swings (pages 16 and 17)

To hit a moving object a gun must almost always be fired at a point ahead of the target; this distance ahead is called the 'lead' and it can be calculated if sufficient time and data are available. If the correct lead is known the shooter can *intercept* as shown in figure 1.

Or he can make a *forward allowance* as shown in figure 2. The correct lead is maintained by swinging the gun through an arc and the gun is fired at any time during the swing. One fundamental weakness is that the correct lead is seldom known.

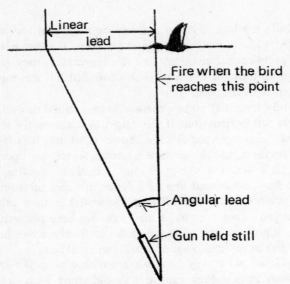

Figure 1. The intercept method

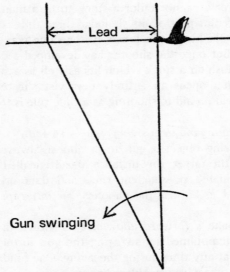

Figure 2. Forward allowance

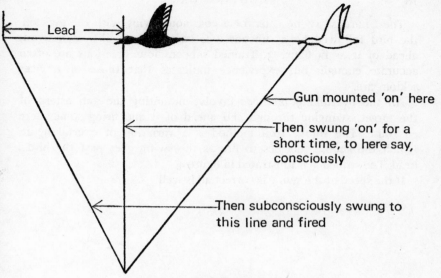

Figure 3. The Churchill swing

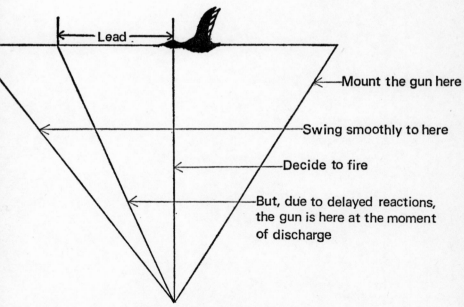

Figure 4. The smoke trail method

B

The *Churchill swing* calls for a conscious swing with the gun 'on' the bird followed by a subconscious swing (Churchill's own word) ahead of it as in figure 3. Trained subconscious reactions are often accurate enough, but experience indicates that those of novices seldom are.

All the *overtaking methods* involve mounting the gun astern of the target, swinging through and ahead of it and firing somewhere en route. The *smoke trail* method is a variation of overtaking in which the shooter decides to fire as the swing goes past the bird's head. The sequence is illustrated in figure 4.

If the speed of the swing is correct all is well.

2

Shall I be Good Enough?

Average skill with a shotgun does not demand a start in childhood and a lifetime spent in green places, but neither is it something which can be acquired without application. Starting in childhood is an advantage, but a latecomer can make up the ground very quickly and many men who hardly saw a gun before their fiftieth birthday have become better than average shots within two years. Or perhaps I should say that they had more than average skill with a gun, because a knowledge of the ways of game, which is part of a good shot's education, takes longer to learn. Outstanding skill is probably beyond the reach of a late starter, and all the great performers were probably blessed with great natural talent and shot an exceptional amount from childhood.

Skill with a gun is something which repays the effort of learning, for it stays with one right into old age and improves all the way. Rugby football becomes too exhausting soon after the age of thirty, at forty the falls inseparable from steeplechasing become more than the frame can endure and power leaves the golfer in his fifties; but shooting does not fade with the years—it matures and improves. A grandfather is often the best shot of three generations with a stalwart grandson in third place.

Most men can undoubtedly become tolerable shots though it must be admitted that some are born to be duffers with a gun, just as those born tone-deaf will never become musicians, but the number of incurable duffers is much smaller than is generally supposed. A secret course of lessons has transformed many men who despaired of reaching an acceptable standard into useful shots and thus opened the joys of the shooting field to them. Shooting is not a competitive sport, and nothing spoils the fun more quickly than an element of competition, but one must reach a certain standard to be acceptable and, as I shared the secret of those lessons several times, I was particularly glad to see the result. The only would-be shooters I have known who failed to cross the Rubicon were either arthritic, asthmatic, very excitable or extremely prone to gun-headaches.

Defective eyesight is only a handicap if a man cannot distinguish between a partridge and a pheasant at a distance of sixty yards; an ability to play games is an advantage in that it usually implies good physical co-ordination and a sense of balance; but these can be developed and many men who have lost an arm or a leg have learned to shoot well. It might be thought that a good physique and quick reflexes were an advantage, but experience does not bear this out, and a receptive mind and the wish to learn are really more important.

Shyness is responsible for keeping away many men who would enjoy shooting. Sometimes they think that twenty years of commuting with a minimum of physical activity have put dexterity in wet woodlands beyond their reach. More often, having tried their hands and found that game eluded their shot, they believe the stupid legend that most men can shoot well by instinct and that the others can never learn. I do not subscribe to that belief and am firmly of the opinion that good shots are made rather than born. A certain tenacity of purpose is essential, enthusiasm at week-ends is not enough, and the novice must submit to the instructor. That is the essence of the matter, submission to an informed teacher and perseverence: given these two things almost anyone can become a better than average shot. And I say better than average after due thought: it is not a mathematical impossibility for most to be better than the average, for the average shooting man neither takes lessons nor practises, and the general standard reflects this.

No golfer would expect to play to his handicap after putting his clubs aside for six months, nor would a cricketer hope to make runs if he had not touched a bat since the previous season, yet men will blithely clean a gun they have not seen for seven months and expect to shoot well with it. Of course they do not shoot well, we humans are not made like that, since any form of dexterity calls for constant practice and the man who comes to the first shoot sharpened by practice has an advantage equivalent to a stroke a hole at golf. That is why so many people can be above the average—if they will bestir themselves.

The best route to proficiency is probably a judicious mixture of professional instruction, reading, practice without firing and thought. It is self-evident that the instructor and the book must teach the same method and that a gun must be beside the reader, but it is less obvious that scraps of advice from random sources should be avoided. The danger is that there is more than one 'correct' way of shooting and an item from one method, though good in itself, should never be grafted onto another. Perhaps an informed novice should be allowed to choose the method he wishes to learn, but once the choice has been made he should stick to it in the undiluted form. Only when he can hold his own with the field should he even consider modifications.

Shooting running game with a rifle has something in common with using a shotgun, but the skills and physical attributes of the rifleman who lies down and fires at fixed targets are so different that proficiency on a rifle range is no indication of potential skill with a gun. I do not maintain, as some people do, that experience with a rifle is a disadvantage to a novice with a gun, but I think that they are as separate and distinct as, say, sailing and rowing a boat.

Women can shoot just as well as men if only they will use guns suited to their size and strength. All too often they form the fixed opinion that guns are heavy, cumbersome things which kick painfully, because they first fire a gun well-suited to their husband or brother but ill-adapted to anyone smaller, be they man or woman. They never learn that a properly selected and fitted gun has little weight and, when correctly mounted, has no recoil at all. The cartridge does all the hard work in shooting while the firer only mounts and swings the gun, as long as it is the right gun and a good fit.

Finally I would restate my belief that almost anyone can become a fair shot. Admittedly there are exceptions, but the vast majority have only to make an effort for a few months and it need not cost very much. On the other hand the task should not be made to seem easier than it is: the novice must do his own learning although the instructor can inform and correct him. The pupil must first absorb the teaching with his brain and then transform it into reflex actions by practice, practice and more practice. There just are no short cuts.

3

Choosing a Shooting School

My own experience could not have been happier but bad schools exist, and were I seeking a school for my novice son in a strange land I should look for one whose graduates had a neat, effective style. A high tower and other adequate equipment are essential and something very like the smoke trail method must be taught, for forward allowance is of limited use and I profoundly distrust shooting by flair alone. A sound technique, once learned, lasts for a lifetime and is a firm base in times of trouble. A loss of form is not a catastrophe then for, though brilliance departs, the man never sinks below the level of a sound workman and his confidence is not shattered. In practice he soon recovers his form if he knows how to go about curing himself.

It is undoubtedly the instructor who makes or mars the school. The cost of cartridges and clays being equal for all schools, the fashionable establishments do not charge a great deal more than those which are less well known, but the instructors vary. That three of the greatest instructors I have known were all outstanding shots is immaterial; a good instructor is not necessarily a good shot, and an excellent shot may be a poor instructor. A good instructor must know his subject, which includes fitting guns, but the vital thing is that he should be able to *communicate* with his pupils, and to do this he must be an articulate man with the knack of conveying his meaning—he must also be more than something of a practical psychologist.

If I were choosing for my son I should be inclined to have a lesson myself and then watch the boy's lesson very closely. Then I should either go elsewhere or place the pupil in the instructor's hands without qualification or reserve, just as I should with a surgeon.

A junior instructor, speaking from the heart, once enquired how he should cope with a novice who insisted on teaching him. The advice he received was to the effect that the pupil who did not try to teach the instructing staff something was rare indeed, but if he did not do his homework it was better to get rid of him before he gave the school a bad reputation.

4

A Neat Style from the Outset

Try to cultivate a good style from the very beginning; its value will become apparent later. Remember that every movement is a possible source of error so eliminate all unnecessary movements and curtail those which are essential. Eventually you will have to move very fast indeed but at this stage you should concentrate on smooth, precise movements with your balance nicely maintained at all times. Every beginner uses much more force than is necessary to move his gun about and tries to gain speed by having his muscles much too tense, but this defeats his own purpose. He will get far, far better results by relaxing, striving for smooth repetition of exactly the same movement each time, while employing no more strength than is necessary to keep the gun under accurate control.

Do not do anything to the limit of your strength, but keep an ample margin in reserve. Set the muscles of the jaw and neck when firing but do not clench your teeth as hard as you can, for this sets up a general tension and makes it impossible for the other muscles to work smoothly and in unison. For the same reason do not exaggerate anything but try for the middle of the road with plenty of room for adjustment in either direction. If you have room for adjustments and keep your balance, you will avoid the awkward, contorted positions from which it is quite impossible to shoot accurately.

Very few of us really do what we think we do, so it is wise to practise in front of a long looking-glass. Home-movie films can also be very helpful.

Although there is a temptation to look at the muzzle of the gun as you bring it to your shoulder, try to focus your eyes firmly on your target before you move your gun at all and to keep them glued on the mark until after the shot has been fired. You will see the muzzle just as you see the front part of the car you are driving, but from the very beginning form the habit of looking hard at the target and ignoring everything else.

As to whether you should look at the target with both eyes open or whether you should close the left eye there can be no fixed rule. In general I go with the majority and prefer that the shooter should keep both eyes open, but I never insist if the novice closes one eye instinctively. He may be correcting a fault of vision, and many people come to shotguns after playing with air guns, or learning to use rifles in the armed forces, so that they close one eye from force of habit. All these people will drop the habit if it is beneficial to do so and no-one has really mastered the art unless he can shoot in both styles. If the right eye is only slightly the master and it tires, the left eye will take over and then it must be closed. Also, with a grossly ill-fitting gun there is no alternative to aiming it like a rifle, with one eye shut, and swinging it ahead of the bird.

I repeat that I prefer to see both eyes open but the importance of this point is often overstressed; the great virtue may be that it tends to stop the shooter aiming his gun like a rifle, but it does not make much practical difference apart from this. Though it is heresy to some I invite them to shoot clays in both styles and to compare the scores afterwards: mine never seem to be very different. The decisive advantage may be that it enables some people, but only some, to see an oncoming bird throughout its flight even though the muzzle has been swung between the master eye and the bird. The curious fact that some, but not all, of those who shoot with both eyes open can do this offers a choice of techniques for shooting oncoming birds which is examined in detail later in the book.

5

Holding and Mounting the Gun

Even experienced men should take a critical look at the way they hold their guns, for errors creep in insidiously and are a common cause of loss of form.

The right hand should be a trifle under the small of the stock with the back of the hand turned clockwise until it is past the vertical. The trigger should be pressed with the pad of the fore-finger, rather than with the wrinkle under the joint, as this will bring the second finger well clear of the trigger guard and the bruises it can give. The thumb *must* be curled round the small of the stock: if it lies along the top it can suffer painful damage from the end of the lever. The real test of the correctness of the grip of the right hand is whether the gun can be mounted easily without muscular constraint, without raising the right elbow far and without slackening the grip.

With the grip of the right hand correct, take hold of the fore-end with the left and jiggle the gun up and down with both hands. Slide the left hand fore and aft until the gun balances at its best and then grasp it. If all is ideal the left hand is now the correct distance from the muzzle and the front of the fore-end will be in the cup of the hand, but we will come back to that in a moment. The left thumb should lie on the side of the barrel to assist pointing; the fingers should curl round the barrel but neither their tips nor the ball of the hand should be high above the sides. A bad fault is to let them get near the rib and obstruct the view. The importance of not rotating the gun in either direction is shown up by the notion that if a gun had sights, as a rifle has, they would have to be kept upright. To cant the barrel sideways is to ensure a miss.

The grip should be firm but not rigid; as with a golfer's grip of his club the tightness should be the minimum necessary for control. The arms must work smoothly, accurately, quickly and in unison, and any rigidity makes this difficult if not impossible.

Much bad shooting with the second barrel is caused by failure to divide the recoil equally between the left and right sides of the body. Ideally the left arm should take such a share that the body is rotated in neither direction by the kick. The left hand should be pushing forward towards the target from the instant mounting begins until after firing, and this will ensure that it takes its proper share of the recoil.

So much for holding the gun—now for mounting it. Fix your eyes on some mark and allow both hands to point the gun in its general direction by the light of nature, then push the left hand towards the target; the right hand goes forward and upwards at the start of mounting, sliding the butt along the coat, then it pulls back to bed the butt into the shoulder. At the instant of firing the gun should be stretched between the left hand pushing forward and the right hand pulling back.

Novices should ensure that the butt is bedded firmly into the shoulder every time, for this ensures that the gun cannot get up speed from the recoil before striking the firer. Advanced shooting demands that the gun should sometimes be fired before the butt has reached the shoulder, but trained men can cut corners in ways no beginner should risk.

The 'ready' position

You should now mount your gun from a 'ready' position between the relaxed posture in which you will spend the bulk of the time and the final position with the gun mounted for firing. Adopt this ready position by holding the gun with the hands as they will be when firing, but with the fore-finger *not* on the trigger, and clamp the stock between the upper arm and the side. Hold the muzzle safely high or low in accordance with the target expected and, at the same time, face the direction from which the game is expected and take the correct stance. Stance is described in the next chapter.

Now you are ready for instant action and you mount the gun in the manner described already, pushing forward with the left hand and sliding the butt up the coat with the right, while keeping your eyes glued to the target. The time to come from the relaxed position to the ready is at the first hint of action: when a pheasant's wings are heard, when a keeper blows his whistle or when your dog shows an interest in something in a hedge.

Some men slide the safety catch forward as they come to the ready position but it is really better to do this while mounting.

One of the fundamentals of mounting a gun correctly is that the butt should be brought to exactly the same place on the shoulder every single time. The method just described helps to ensure this; it is also the quickest and the most reliable in most shooting situations. There are other methods and, when you are pressed for time, the gun can be mounted directly from a relaxed position.

The 'ready' position
Figure 5

The first quiet practice

It is called quiet practice because snap caps take the place of cart-ridges and, having read to this point, the novice should now drive the lessons home by practising in front of a long looking-glass. Every-thing will be new and strange, and he will use far more force than is necessary, but he should try for smooth precision first and let speed come when practice brings dexterity. Let him load with snap caps, come from the waiting stance to the ready position, mount the gun on the reflection of his own right eye, squeeze the trigger, reload and repeat the drill.

The importance of quiet practice cannot be exaggerated; only when any lesson has been practised to the point at which it has become a sub-conscious reaction is the novice ready for the next lesson.

The real object is to learn co-ordination, and it is a lengthy process, but it is quite unnecessary to fire live cartridges all the time. Swallows and bats in the garden or waders flying along the water's edge are admirable for quiet practice with an unloaded gun, and there is no better way of learning to shoot than to do such practice between serious lessons. It cannot be repeated too often that the substance of the first lesson should be driven into the sub-conscious by practice before the second lesson is attempted, but there is a word of warning which should be heeded. The home student must be prepared to un-learn bad habits picked up in the intervals between lessons, and the backsight should be taken off any rifle used in practice, to avoid forming the habit of aiming.

Pupils vary so widely that no-one can predict how long it will take to progress beyond the novice stage, or how many or how few lessons will be necessary. Aptitude plays a part in the pace at which a student advances, but the decisive thing in the standard he ultimately reaches is his perseverance with practice, subject always to his natural talent, of course. An absolute beginner who did his homework would prob-ably be acceptable in the shooting field after six lessons, knowledge of game apart, but he might well be surpassed by a real enthusiast who set to with a friend, studied this book and did five minutes' quiet practice every day, fired some thirty cartridges every week but never went to a shooting school.

6

Stance

Everyone feels clumsy during the first spells of quiet practice, but after a few minutes' drill every day for several days the novice can answer the vital question, 'Is your grip comfortable?' At the outset he was in the same state as the novice horseman who is told to put the stirrups at a comfortable length but finds that no comfort exists. When he has become familiar with the basically correct grip he is allowed to make some adjustments. The right hand may be rotated a trifle in either direction, provided that its grip on the stock is firm and that the upper arm is at an angle of at least ten degrees below the horizontal when the gun is mounted. The left hand may be tromboned up and down the barrel provided that it is neither perfectly straight nor extravagantly bent.

Because H.M. King George V shot with his left arm straight it became the 'done thing', but it was a mannerism which is a disadvantage to most of us. Avoid mannerisms if you can and avoid exaggerations; comfort will come with use, and the simplest possible style, right in the middle of the road, is the objective at this stage.

The boxer's stance

As soon as the gun can be mounted comfortably the novice should learn the boxer's stance, which is the one to use whenever the gun is at an angle of less than 45 degrees above the horizontal. The illustration facing page 32 shows most of the essentials but notice that the bulk of the weight is on the left foot, that the body is inclined forward and that the right heel may, or may not, leave the ground.

As you come into this stance from the ready position and start to mount your gun, have the feeling that you are dabbing a tentative straight left on to the target. Some instructors say 'Bayonet the bird', others say 'Point the left hand at the bird', but the difference is only in the form of words. The important thing is that the hands play a vital role during the early stages of mounting: not only do they point the barrels in the general direction of the target but they can be trained to such a pitch that men can, and do, shoot game when the hands rather than the eyes tell them to fire. However, that is advanced shooting and for the moment it does not matter which phrase you choose provided that you focus your eyes on the target and direct the gun towards it with both hands, while mounting the gun in the manner described already. There is less room for error if the left foot goes out first and the gun is mounted afterwards, although a trained man can do both together if necessary.

Standing thus, the bulk of the swing for an oncoming bird can be done with the arms alone, but the novice should bend his whole body from the ankles up. This is essential when the gun goes past the vertical, and it is as well to have one method rather than two.

The close stance

This is the stance to use whenever the gun is more than 45 degrees above the horizontal.

To get the feet into place just go into the boxer's stance and pull the left foot back until the heel is two inches in front of the right heel and three or four inches to its left. To remove doubt here is an alternative method. Stand to attention facing north; move the left foot three or four inches sideways and two inches forward; keep the ball of the right foot still but shuffle the right heel until you are comfortable. You are now placed to shoot targets rather west of north.

More than half of your weight should be on your right foot and the bulk of its share should be on the *heel*.

You may feel that this position is awkward at first, but you will find that perseverance is worthwhile if you take this stance, with a gun in your hands, and swing as you would for an oncoming bird, allowing your left heel to rise. The average shooter's gun comes well past the vertical quite readily. Now take the boxer's stance, with your weight on the forward foot, and swing up and back again. The gun will not come back nearly so far, will it?

To move from one stance to the other simply slide the left foot forward or back.

The reader would be well-advised to make a mental note at this point that these two stances are really teaching devices. In fact there is only one stance, but it is infinitely variable and too difficult to learn in one step. I return to this subject in chapter 15.

Figure 6
The classic position for a bird overhead. Notice that the bulk of the weight is on the right heel, that the left heel rises and that the whole body from the ankles up bends without loss of balance.

Figure 7
The position for a high bird on the right. The weight has gone to the right and the hips and shoulders slide round level.

... and with the gun rather steeper. Note that the left foot has come back a little, that the body is a trifle more upright and that a smaller fraction of the weight is on the left foot.

The boxer's stance with the gun horizontal ...

A turn to the left in three phases. Here the man is watching an oncoming target over the muzzles in what is essentially the 'ready' position.

The first movement of the turn: the butt has been lowered and the muzzle raised for safety, the left foot has slid back in an arc and the hips and shoulders have come round level. Notice that his eyes

Then he twists on the ball of his right foot and takes a shot behind him without loss of balance.

Turning in either stance

From the close stance most people can shoot accurately with their guns well behind the vertical, but it is a mistake to fire when the gun is close to the limit of the swing. The resistance of the muscles as they approach the limit, backwards or sideways, forbids accuracy, so you should turn in plenty of time.

Turning is so simple that many people do not trouble to learn it properly, with the result that they never shoot nearly as well as they might. To turn to the left just slide the left foot back in an arc and twist on the ball of the right foot. To turn to the right slide the right foot back in an arc and twist on the ball of the left foot.

Never allow one shoulder to sink below the other as you turn, because this will cant the gun to one side and ensure a miss.

More quiet practice

You will probably have to work quite hard before all these new positions and movements become sub-conscious reactions done smoothly, quickly and correctly. Golfers, boxers and dancers learn more quickly than most of us because they have already taught their feet to do one thing while their arms do another and their attention is concentrated on a third. Each item can be learned easily in front of a looking-glass but combining them, and doing several things at the same time, does take time and will-power.

Many short sessions are more rewarding than a few long periods; do not hurry, and keep your balance all the time while going through everything you have been taught so far in every permutation you can think of. The grip, ready position, mounting the gun while dabbing a straight left onto the target, the two stances and the turns are the most important, but if you include pressing the triggers and reloading so much the better.

Always practise with some specific point in mind, for to go through the motions with your mind in neutral is useless. Always bring your gun up onto a mark at which you are looking hard: the importance of this will emerge later.

7

Feet and Head

In chapter 6 the reader was introduced to the elements of footwork and the usual reaction to its mention is 'But what about the wild-fowler who must shoot with his feet anchored in mud?' True enough, he must, and the obvious reply is that I am trying to make things easy for the beginner who can learn the difficult things later. But it goes deeper than that, for no-one can approach his full potential without footwork to match the rest of his skill. There is a lot of wrong thinking on this subject and I should like to state another point of view.

If you plant your feet correctly for one shot, say for a low bird in front, the difficulty is reduced; if you fail to move them every other shot becomes more difficult than it need be. In this case it is almost impossible to hit a bird directly overhead and those high up on either side become much harder. Every form of manual dexterity, be it golf, shooting, billiards or sawing down a line, is performed most accurately when the man is comfortably poised and free from muscular constraint, and the man who avoids all constraint has a very big advantage. However, the variety of shots in practice is so great, and the time available is so short, that the avoidance of all constraint is hardly possible. One school of thought adopts a middle of the road stance, which is more or less correct for quite a variety of shots, and reaps the rewards and penalties of compromise: the follower of this school is reasonably good at certain shots but ineffective at others. The other school of thought, to which I subscribe, holds that although all constraint cannot be avoided it can be minimized by even fair footwork. Further, this footwork can be learned so easily, and pays such a handsome dividend, that the shooter who disdains it has a strange sense of values. It is not quite true to say that no shot is difficult if you have enough time to take up the ideal stance but it is largely true. The men who will not move their feet can be recognized from the fantastic, contorted positions they get themselves into; sometimes they lose their balance altogether.

Shooting two partridges from one covey is well within the scope of all of us; to kill three calls for sound footwork, while to take four demands the footwork of a boxer, if not of a dancer. But why not at least try to join the *élite* who sometimes get five? Throughout your shooting life remember that the shot goes much faster than any bird and that there is almost always time to take the extra step which will put your feet into the right place. Sometimes you will be compelled to fire with the wrong foot in front, but it will not be very often if you train your feet during quiet practice.

The position of the head

Provided that one avoids the two extremes of ducking down onto the stock, as a rifleman does, and drawing back the head, as a boxer may sway back from a punch, it does not matter precisely where the head is held provided that (a) it is in exactly the same place every time and (b) once there its position remains absolutely constant *in relation to the shoulder*. That the shoulder may be turning does not affect the issue, the head must go with the shoulder as that of a statue does.

A good position is that of a stylish boxer as he shoots out the classic straight left, and if you find this comfortable and natural make it yours, but you will lose nothing if you cleave to something slightly different. The slight turn of the head to the right with its inclination forward can be seen in the photograph facing page 32.

Most of the difficulty of keeping the head still will disappear if you look hard at the target while mounting the gun, for then the head will reach its final position and freeze relative to the shoulder before the gun has moved far, and the stock will be brought up to the cheek. Notice that carefully: the stock should be brought up towards the cheek, not the reverse. It is important that the woodwork should come not onto the jawbone or the cheekbone but between them, where there will be no bruising. If your first gun is a reasonably correct fit this is only a matter of adopting a slightly different position for your head, but if this does not suffice the stock must be altered.

Now consider what has happened: the butt is always in the same place on your shoulder, the hands are directing the barrels at the point on which your eyes are fixed and your eyes are always in the same place relative to your shoulder—or to the rib of the gun if it is easier to think of it in that way. If you press the trigger of a well-fitted gun without taking aim, the pattern will be centred on the point at which you are looking. Your eyes supervise but they should not aim the gun.

If the gun does not fit the barrels will be directed, not at the point at which you are looking, but at the same angle from it every time. The final fitting of the gun removes this constant error so that, human fallibility apart, the properly-mounted gun points wherever the man is looking.

Sceptics may doubt that gunmakers can tailor stocks so accurately but, give or take a few hundredths of an inch, they make light of the task. The tiny residual error is soon eradicated by the adaptability of the body. Young, supple bodies can adapt themselves to quite large errors although their elders need more exact fitting.

People hesitate to believe that their hands will point wherever their eyes are focused but they can be reassured by making this simple test. Keeping the head still, look hard at some object and then point one forefinger at it; now sight along the finger to see if the alignment was correct. It always is correct, provided that the head did not move, because our hands do so many things in the ordinary course of living that they work with great precision.

The imperative need for keeping the head still while mounting the gun becomes clear if the test is repeated while the head is moving, for it is then seen that all accuracy is lost.

8

The First Clays

If the novice has fired a few shots at some stationary target he will
have learned the feeling of the recoil and the size of the pattern well
enough to try his hand at clays. He should stand close behind the
trap while the clays are thrown low down and straight away from
him. As his gun will be at a flat angle he should use the boxer's stance.
All he has to do is to fix his eyes on the clay, following the slight
rise and fall of its flight, start mounting his gun as soon as he sees
the clay, but without hurrying, and go to it with a brave heart. Let
him reproduce whatever tempo he learned in quiet practice and fire
at his first choice come what may.

Even though everything is new and strange a novice often breaks
these clays from the outset, but he should not be depressed if Fortune
does not smile. He should relax, check the grip and stance, go through
the motions without firing a few times and try again. As soon as
he quietens the butterflies in his tummy the drill he learned during
quiet practice will assert itself and he will hit most of the clays.

Then he should go ahead and enjoy himself, smash them to the
limit of his purse or inclination, for as long as he does not cheat by
aiming the gun he is doing nothing but good. Confidence is mounting,
the handling of the gun is improving; most important of all the co-
ordination of eyes, brain and muscle is growing. This co-ordination,
which maintains the balance while the feet do one thing, the
hands another and the eye is kept on the target, is the bed rock
of shooting and the slowest part to develop. It must be fostered until
the whole becomes a sub-conscious routine done correctly although

the main attention is directed elsewhere; and the only way to cultivate it is by *practice, practice and more practice*.

The beginner will not be 'all right on the night' if he scamps the practice. Only the fraction which has become sub-conscious will be available at the moment of truth, and whether this fraction is called 'muscle memory' or 'trained reflexes' is unimportant. What matters is the ability to make all the movements correctly, without need of adjustment and without thinking about them. It is said that H.M. King George V kept a gun in his bedroom so that he could practice without firing whenever he wished. He was one of the outstanding shots of his day and if he found it beneficial surely most of us would improve by doing the same.

To return to firing at your first choice. This should be printed indelibly on the mind : never hesitate, make corrections, have second thoughts or dither. However misguided your first choice may have been it might have had rhythm, the others will be worse for they can have none. Do not be afraid of missing, but go about the task with sober confidence knowing that no-one is born able to shoot but that you are one of the great majority who can learn to shoot well enough if given a little time.

Above all do not be shy about shooting less than perfectly in the rather overwhelming surroundings of a shooting school. Remember that the instructor has undoubtedly seen much bad shooting both by absolute beginners and by veterans of the shooting field. He has probably formed some opinion of the state of your shooting education from the way you mounted your gun the very first time and he knows that you will rise to an acceptable standard if only you will let him guide you. Most instructors have a device or two for restraining a pupil who gets a little above himself, but the man they can help the least is the man who is so shy that he does not have a go at the matter. I once saw a better than average shot fire twenty-five cartridges without getting a single hit; his dog curled up behind him and pretended to be asleep; the language he used was unsuitable for the drawing-room but it did not do any good at all. I could see plainly that he was shooting over the top of every single bird, but the real point is that if a more than useful man can do this, and we all have a bad patch sometimes, why should a novice be ashamed of missing a few clays? After all it would not really matter if you contrived to miss fifty consecutive shots, would it? However, if you do your quiet practice you will almost certainly kill your share, and perhaps a trifle more than your share.

Although I have written of clays and given the impression that everything except quiet practice took place at a shooting school this was only for clarity. Real clays thrown from a trap are ideal but there are lots of inexpensive substitutes. Clays can be thrown by hand from a special stick, and beer-can projectors are on the market; old gramophone records are excellent and windfall apples will serve, while old tennis balls hit with a racket or a cricket bat meet most needs. An inventive boy arranged a sloping wire down which a target slid on a pulley, like a chair on a ski-lift, and model aeroplanes have been engaged in duels with air guns. Anything which flies smoothly will serve as a clay, and there is no limit to invention. The gun need not necessarily be a shotgun, for an air rifle can be very instructive if it is fired at a target from a bridge or low bank with water as a background so that the splash can be seen.

9

The Smoke Trail Method

It is at this point that the method which I advocate branches off from the others and follows a course of its own. It is roughly parallel to Robert Churchill's, and not so far from it that you cannot cut across from one to the other very quickly, but it gets further and further away from Forward Allowance. Whichever method you choose everything you have learned already is common to all three systems and you have not wasted your time.

Let us get the two exceptions out of the way and then come to the heart of the whole problem of shooting any moving thing. One exception is the bird which is flying straight towards the gun and would pass up the barrel if it continued its course; the other is the bird on an exactly opposite course away from the gun. Just shoot straight at these birds and dismiss them from your mind.

Now imagine that every other moving object at which you wish to shoot is leaving a trail of smoke as an aeroplane sometimes does. Just fix your eyes on the trail, mount the gun properly, swing smoothly up the trail, press the trigger as you go past the bird's head and go on swinging with a long, smooth follow-through. You will probably hit the bird but, should you miss, just swing up the trail again smoothly, bravely and a trifle faster than before. Quite soon you will be getting a fair number of hits and, as you get the feel of things, mount the gun close behind the bird rather than a long way down the trail.

I do not want to break the sequence of thought by explaining all the mathematics now, as that will be gone into later for those who are interested, but very briefly, while the gun is swung smoothly up the trail it is gathering data and while swinging ahead of the bird it is predicting its future path from that data. Although the eyes give the signal to fire as the swing goes past the head there is a tiny interval of time while brain muscle and trigger mechanism react and, during that fraction of a second, the muzzle swings ahead of the bird, which is why you must go on swinging.

Notice particularly that the speed of the swing is the only variable in the whole method. Whether the bird be fast or slow, near or far, crossing, climbing, diving, oncoming or anything else, if it is moving at all just mount your gun on the trail, swing up it, press the trigger as you go past the head and follow through. The only question is 'How fast should the swing be?' and, though practice alone can give the answer, in general a fast bird needs a fast swing and a slow bird a slow one. The man should react to the tempo set by the bird. A crow loafing along is overtaken by a leisurely swing, a crossing pheasant inspires some urgency, and the sight of a teal at full speed down wind is so thrilling that the whole body may take charge and swing the gun through a big angle very quickly. Only practice can find the answer, for each of us is different in this respect, and crossing shots at the height of first-floor windows are excellent for the purpose.

One of their virtues for our present purpose is that generally speaking the speed of the swing which will keep a gun on a plain crossing bird is constant for practical purposes. During all practice from this stage onwards try to achieve a fluid, smooth swing which accelerates evenly from the start, all the way up the trail, to a point well past the bird. Every golfer is familiar with this striving for a strong, relaxed and rhythmical swing and knows that he does best when he pushes fear aside and uses less than his maximum effort; this is very true of shooting also.

Always stand in the ready position until you see the clay, but then start moving to the correct stance, mounting the gun and swinging at the same moment. Do not fall into the common error of making three separate movements in sequence, but combine them and do them all at the same time. This is so important that beginners are allowed to jump the gun and start when they hear the trap spring, for a certain deliberation is necessary for accuracy. If you feel pressed for time do remember that the pellets go much faster than any clay; imagine that a witch doctor has added thirty years to your age, and move at the speed of the older man who is content to let the pellets hurry for him. Also bear constantly in mind that smoothness is essential, for without it the underlying mathematics are done wrongly.

It is better to fire no more than ten cartridges at any one stand. After some crossing shots try some more going straight away and thrown a few degrees to either side of straight before returning to crossing shots.

Very few beginners miss by shooting ahead of the bird and, when this does happen, the mistake is usually obvious. So if performance falls off after a series of hits swing faster rather than slower up the trail, but if this does not bring a cure check the grip, the stance and the position of the head and ensure that the head does not move. Quite often the fault will be found at the end of the line: although you thought that you fired before checking the swing the reverse was true so that there was no follow-through. The other great cause of missing is moving the head: we all do it sometimes and the only remedy is to try a little harder.

Beginners seem to take to the smoke trail method more readily than to any other and probably the reason for this is that they have only one variable quantity to cope with. They need not fear that they are venturing upon a new and untried path because the method has been proved in the fire of experience over many years, although I gave it its name quite recently as a result of seeing an aeroplane's contrail in the sky and thinking how much easier it was to imagine such a trail from a game bird than to 'swing along the line of the bird' —although this phrase describes exactly the same action. Nor need they fear that, having been at great pains to learn the method, they will ever be asked to discard it and learn something better. Many men remain smoke trailers for life but it is very easy to switch to Robert Churchill's method once a tolerable standard has been reached via the smoke trail; also it is very simple for experienced forward allowancers and Churchill swingers to use the smoke trail and I invite them to try for the fun of it. This is not an attempt to make unwilling converts, but if they will devote even twenty cartridges to the purpose they may well come to the conclusion that the method really does have its virtues. I do not claim that it is the best for all men and all shots, no one method can be that, but it is a very good all-round system peculiarly well suited to beginners.

10

Oncoming Birds

The basic technique of swinging up the smoke trail and firing as the swing goes past the bird's head remains sound, as it does for every single shot at any moving object, but there are difficulties which can cause dissension if a plea for tolerance is not heeded. The point is that we humans vary greatly where our eyes are concerned and what is true of one excellent shot may be quite untrue of another. It is common knowledge that many of us live a full span without ever realizing that we were colour blind all the time; it is less well known that double vision lurks, unsuspected, in some of us and that all sorts of peculiarities exist in honest, upright and congenial men with whom we should be delighted to go shooting. Let us recognize that these differences exist and that those who claim to have greater or lesser powers than our own are not necessarily either boastful or incompetent, but are just different.

The particular point at issue is that some people who shoot with both eyes open can see the target clearly at all times even when the muzzle has swung between the master eye and the bird. Others, with both eyes open, only see the target vaguely when the master eye's view is obstructed and others lose sight of it completely. Now let us be clear about this : a shooter who closes his disengaged eye must lose sight of the bird, unless he moves his head, but some men who keep both eyes open also lose sight of it while others do not. I have heard several explanations of this undoubted fact but never one that carried much conviction. Perhaps I had better declare my interest, because I see the bird at all times with a single-barrelled gun but lose sight of it with a side-by-side double-barrel.

Those who see the bird clearly at all times can maintain the correct relationship between the muzzle and the target so, if they wish, they can use forward allowance, but anyone who loses sight of the target must find a way to hit a mark which he cannot see at the moment of firing. The answer is so delightfully simple that I often marvel that anyone should concern himself with the complexities of forward allowance when a much easier solution is at hand. All you have to do is to mount the gun a trifle behind the bird, that is to say below it, swing up the smoke trail and fire as the bird's head is blacked out by the muzzle. Just swing and fire when the head disappears. Now let us put the matter to the test.

The first oncoming clays should be thrown low to pass over the gun, and the shooter must realize that the swing it not at a constant pace but accelerates from dead slow, when the clay is far off and the gun is at a flat angle, to a great pace as the gun goes past the vertical. You will catch the rhythm of the swing if some clays are thrown directly over your head and the gun is swung on them throughout their flight, for you will feel an acceleration clearly. The acceleration required to hit the target is a trifle faster than the one you felt.

At the risk of repetition, the novice has only to mount his gun a trifle behind these birds and swing up the trail, firing as the muzzle blots out the head, to do very well. He will do very well indeed if he takes them early, with the clay far in front and the gun almost horizontal. The reason for this is that the gun is flat, so that the swing is slow and little lead is required, the spread of the pattern covering all but major error. Furthermore the clay must travel down much of the length of the column of shot in the air and is more likely to be struck than when crossing its diameter; with a live target the bird 'walks onto the punch'. Every boxer who has moved towards his opponent's punch instead of 'riding' it (drawing away from the blow) will remember the shattering difference. So, without hurrying, always engage an oncoming target the moment it comes into range.

When you are hitting clays thrown low and directly overhead, vary the shooting by having them thrown up to twenty yards on either side of you and, as practice brings dexterity, position yourself nearer the trap so that you have to move faster, but *never* slur the drill. It is usually at this stage that a novice learns to move from the boxer's to the close stance subconsciously.

These low, oncoming shots are one of the main features of shooting both driven grouse and partridges and they are not difficult if only you have plenty of time to do what you know perfectly well you should do. The difficulty in the field is that you always, or nearly always, have to move faster than you would wish and that the birds upset your programme by taking evasive action.

11

'Tracking' and Some New Exercises

This is an appropriate stage at which to bring some of the loose threads together and to introduce some new ideas. You know that any movement is a possible source of error, so the best plan is to cut out all unnecessary movements and to curtail those which are essential; one of the great movement-reducers is the mounting of the gun in the manner I advocate, for then it is only necessary to slide the butt about six inches up the coat to have it in the correct place. You know also that you should point the barrels at the target with your hands from the moment you start to mount the gun, but now I want you to carry things a little further.

The scheme applies to every shot but it is easiest to describe it if we imagine a low oncoming bird flying towards you in plain sight from a great distance. You see this bird when it is still far out of range and you have all the time you need, so you fix your eyes on it and come to the ready position, and this is where you learn something new. Even though the bird is still out of range, allow your hands to point the muzzle at the bird and to follow its every movement; keep your eyes fixed on the bird, pick up its line and speed, and let yourself react to its movement until it comes into range; then mount the gun and fire in the ordinary way. The new factors to emphasize are picking up the target with eye and muzzle before mounting starts and following its movement closely. I call this 'tracking' the target, and it is very like following a partner who is leading you in a waltz, although it is even more like allowing a trusted horse to carry you

46

over a fence. You allow your partner to take the initiative and just follow the movement and tempo with your whole body. When you decide to shoot you only have to slide the butt a few inches upwards and the bird is as good as dead. Shooting in these conditions is very easy indeed once you have learned the knack of tracking.

In practice you seldom have sufficient time to track completely unless the bird is high up, but try to include at least a partial track every time you can. This is an ideal to be striven for rather than a routine measure to be executed without fail, but it is most rewarding and one of the reasons why experts always seem to have plenty of time.

It is necessary at this stage to give the column of shot some thought, because although we tend to think of a pattern of shot moving forward like a plate because we see the holes made in a piece of paper, there is really a column of some length, and a spherical target is more likely to be struck when travelling down its length than when crossing its diameter. Also it does give some margin for error because even if the leading pellets do pass ahead of the bird, the later pellets may well strike it. The ballistics of rifles is a fairly exact science, in which plain statements are accurate, but with shotguns we are dealing with averages and probabilities. Unlike a bullet, a charge of shot can score a theoretical hit which misses because of holes in the pattern, or a theoretical miss which hits because of stray pellets. Specialists have a jargon of their own which enables them to write briefly but precisely of cases like that, but I am writing for laymen and I hope that experts will not take me to task for using ordinary language to make my meaning clear without sacrificing too much accuracy.

Finally to introduce a new and very important exercise into the reader's quiet practice. Let him stand under any horizontal wire, such as a telephone wire or overhead cable, then let him mount his gun on the insulator at one end of the wire before swinging up and back as he would for a high, oncoming bird. The object is to keep the foresight on the wire throughout the swing without letting it wobble off to either side, as well as getting thoroughly familiar with the close stance and with maintaining control of the gun when it has been swung behind the vertical.

At the same time it is a good plan to make a start on learning the very difficult swing which starts with the gun pointing vertically upwards and travels down the wire to the insulator. This swing will be needed for high birds which have passed overhead and most of us have to work for some time before we can do it propery.

A turn to the right. Cp. the photographs facing page 33. Again the muzzle is raised, but the right foot slides back and the hips and shoulders turn about ninety degrees.

The turn completed with the 'wrong' foot in front. If pressed for time he will fire from this position . . .

. . . but if he has time he will move whichever foot is carrying the less weight and shoot from a normal stance. A purist might say that his feet are too wide apart, but his balance is so good and his aggression so evident that no serious fault can be found.

Left: 'Everything Wrong'. This is a most instructive photograph; his feet are placed correctly for a low bird in front, but he has not moved them although his target is now high up and to his left. He cannot slide his hips and shoulders round, so he has hollowed his back and canted the gun to the left. If he fires he will most certainly miss. Both the tight, thick coat and the clumsy boots are serious handicaps, and he would be more comfortable if his over-trousers did not guide the rain into his boots; unless they will be torn by undergrowth it is better to have over-trousers outside the boots.

Right: The shot can be taken without strain or contortion, if the feet are brought together and the hips allowed to turn easily. But I think that the camera has caught the instant after the swing was completed and the man has just begun to lower his gun—the butt seems to be a trifle to the right of its correct position.

12

Higher Oncoming Birds

The novice has taken a great step forward once he has mastered the knack of swinging smoothly and accurately up the smoke trail with his left heel rising and the gun under control when it has swung past the vertical. The technique which enabled him to hit clays thrown to imitate driven partridges is exactly the same as that required to shoot those thrown to represent moderately high, driven pheasants, and it is only restated here to avoid any possibility of error. The drill was to come to the ready position at the first hint of action; on sighting the target track it with your eyes and muzzle until you decide to move; then, in one fluid movement, mount the gun, swing up the trail, fire as the muzzle blots out the bird's head and follow through resolutely.

The amendment to this technique required for higher birds is one of degree only. The stance must be as steady as a rock and everything must be more accurate, since with the gun at a steeper angle there is less margin for error; to offset this is the fact that these birds are usually in sight long enough for you to track them for quite a long time. Most of us have a favourite angle of elevation at which we like to take such shots, a trifle flatter than forty-five degrees above the horizontal being a common favourite, but the principle that they should be engaged as soon as they come into range remains sound for two reasons. First, provided that it is within range, an oncomer is easier to hit at a flat angle, and secondly, should you miss you have more time for the second barrel. It follows that the more heavily-choked barrel should be fired first in these cases, and the man who habitually fires either first in all circumstances is not thinking. For going-away shots the right barrel should be fired first with the choked one in reserve for a longer shot.

Very high pheasants

Although wildfowl are often so high as to be out of range, this is only true of pheasants which take off from a hillside far above the gun. This will be accepted if it is remembered that forty-five yards, the maximum sporting range of a 12-bore fired vertically upwards, is about the height of a building of thirteen or fourteen stories and that an oak tree is seldom more than fifteen yards high. Nevertheless, very high pheasants are difficult for a number of reasons, not the least of which is that they are exceptional, so we do not have much practice at them. Perhaps it is this lack of practice which makes us tend to under-estimate the speed at which they are moving and to decide that this particular bird is only cantering, as it were, although it is really at full speed. Also, they are only within range when the gun is at so steep an angle that the margin for error is at a minimum, but this is cancelled to some extent by the fact that their height brings them into view early on so that the shooter is not hurried. They really provide a test of supreme accuracy rather than of rapid execution.

The ordinary gun's best chance is to treat them as formidable opponents vulnerable to orthodox attack, so take them as soon as they come within range of the left barrel, ensure that the swing does not wobble from side to side and assume that every one of them is a real speed-merchant. You should be determined that if you must miss it shall be in front. Above all, never be taken in by the pheasant which is gliding on motionless wings: that bird is sliding down a slope in the air and is probably not flapping his wings only because he is going too fast to do so. Many, many are missed because the gun is deluded into thinking that they are at half speed.

Some of the methods which experts sometimes use to cope with these birds are described in chapter 17 on advanced shooting, but non-experts will do better by using an orthodox swing.

13

Does the Oncomer Still Defeat You?

Some men have real difficulty with oncoming birds, particularly when the gun is at a steep angle. Indeed it is the shooting man's equivalent of Euclid's Pons Asinorum, for once across the bridge the man makes effortless progress, but many shoot for decades and never solve the central problem—partly, I suspect, because the problem has never been clearly stated to them. So let me state it now, after begging those whose eyes happen to be different to realize that the other man may be right. Those who have taken this shot in their stride and hit moderately high oncomers as readily as any other shot would probably prefer to skip this chapter and they will lose nothing by doing so.

Now, the bird flies forward as the pellets go up, so the gun must point ahead of the bird at the moment of discharge if they are to collide. Whether you point the gun at the correct spot after estimating a linear distance or an angle, swinging up the smoke trail or any other method, does not alter the fact that, if you hit, the gun was pointing in the only correct direction, so the problem is to find the easiest way of shooting in that direction. The issue is clouded by the fact that some men can see the target clearly even when the muzzle has swung between the master eye and the bird (as it must unless the head is moved), while others lose sight of it. I assume that those who see the bird at all times do so with the disengaged eye, and these people, and these alone, can use forward allowance by maintaining an angular or linear lead if they wish, but they may prefer to join those who lose sight of the target either because they close one eye or for any other reason; these people must learn to hit an object which they cannot see at the time of firing. And that, learning to hit an object which you cannot see at the time of firing, is the central problem. Fortunately, although no-one is born able to solve it, like riding a bicycle, it is easy when you have learned to do it.

Yet men adopt all sorts of stratagems to avoid the issue. Some turn sideways and treat it as an overhead crossing shot, all too many dither, peer and poke while getting into contorted positions from which the finest shot could harm nothing, while some make no attempt to shoot the bird in front but turn round and take a going-away shot. That this is much more difficult is not the chief point; the distressing thing is that all these people are depriving themselves of the most enjoyable part of shooting driven game and substituting misery for pleasure. It is often the nicest men who are in the thickest fog, for they are too shy to ask how they should go about the task and too modest to assume that what the dashing Mr X does easily they too can learn. Above all they will not go near a shooting school, because a strange idea persists that a man, a proper man complete in all particulars, can both shoot and ride well by instinct. Skill with a gun comes to most of us from steady work under the light of intelligence, and very few of us do not benefit from lessons at a good school.

To master the oncomer, it would be wise first to repeat the drill of standing under a horizontal wire and swinging up from the insulator, trying to keep the fore-sight on the wire; it is not difficult to do but it requires a little practice at the outset, and the swing is common to all techniques. Also, without wishing to alarm, it is possible that your right eye is not very much the master and, confused by the muzzle intervening on its line, is losing control to the left eye. This possibility is eliminated by closing the left eye, though a partial closure is usually sufficient.

Forward allowance is probably not seen at its best against oncoming birds but, to be fair, it is true that a man who can see the target clearly throughout its flight can make the correct allowance if he knows what it is. Some opinion of the likelihood of making the correct estimate of the necessary allowance can be gained by reading chapter 18 on the hidden mathematics, but it can be done and I do not wish to dissuade anyone bent on trying.

With the fundamentals as well polished as may be you should fire about twenty shots at moderately high oncoming clays thrown to pass directly over your head by a trap which you can see. This gives you the longest possible look at the clay and I recommend that you should use the smoke trail method because it has only one uncertain quantity—the speed of the swing.

If the results of this trial give you confidence please stick to the method, but there is another if you care to try it. This is set out in detail in Churchill's *Game Shooting* but, for this particular shot, is broadly as follows: grip, stance, ready position and mounting are identical in both Churchill's and the smoke trail method, but the difference starts with the fact that Churchill mounts on the bird; then he swings with it for a fraction of time before speeding up to get in front, and fires when judgment says is proper. Notice that there are two unknowns involved here—how much do you speed up and when do you fire? Churchill advocates swinging as the gun comes up and firing as the butt meets the shoulder, but whether this suits you can only be found by trial. It is an added excellence for some trained men, but some beginners are confused by it.

If you give both methods a fair trial but find that these oncomers still elude the shot, you ought to go to a shooting school which teaches either the smoke trail or Churchill method and put yourself in their hands without reserve, just as you would go to a doctor. You are almost certainly making a consistent fault, possibly your gun does not fit, but you can be quite certain that the instructor will spot what is wrong and put you right if you let him.

14

Over and Past You

Birds which have passed more or less over your head, and are now going away, are a test of footwork in the first instance, but it is also essential that the muzzle of the gun should be safely high or low as you make the turn. What you must never do, even when you are alone, is to allow the gun to be pointed anywhere near where your neighbour would be if you had a neighbour. It is very easy to be concentrating so hard on a partridge which you have seen in front of you but decided to shoot behind that you break this fundamental safety rule. It is better to form a danger-free habit from the outset. More often than not you will point the muzzle steeply upwards, but sometimes it will be downwards, and although either makes the subsequent shot slightly more difficult that is a small matter when compared with the risk you have avoided.

It is important that you should turn quickly and neatly, because there will not be a great deal of time at your disposal, and it is an advantage if you can keep your eye on the bird as you turn, but both are of less importance than avoiding the slightest hint that you are not perfectly safe with a gun.

However, let us assume that you have turned to perfection and that a covey is leaving you low down. You have a perfectly straightforward shot with a family likeness to the first clays you broke, low down and leaving you. Glue your eyes to a particular bird and trust the fit of your gun; pick up the tempo of the swing, up the smoke trail which you imagine coming from the bird of course, but it will be quite slow and of no special difficulty.

By contrast a pheasant which has passed overhead is often considered to be one of the hardest shots there is, only surpassed by its close relative, which is rather to one side and leaving at an angle, as distinct from going straight away.

Part of the difficulty springs from the fact that the swing is produced by an unfamiliar bowing movement which needs practice. This is why you included standing under a horizontal wire and swinging down it, with the gun starting at the vertical and getting flatter as it follows the wire, in your quiet practice. When you can swing in this manner try your hand at some clays, but keep an open mind, because the smoke trail method is at its worst for this particular shot. It will work, but you have to memorize the trail and swing down it, firing as the bird's head appears—at least that is what you must do if you lose sight of the bird. With either forward allowance or the Churchill method the bird is in sight all the time and, although I greatly prefer a beginner to have one method for every single shot, I do not insist if real difficulty is encountered here.

Whatever method is chosen the swing must go with zest; this fact probably lies at the root of the saying that one should shoot at the undercarriage of these birds. Certainly there is no room for half measures, and the swing should go freely right past the bird to a long follow-through, for it is very seldom that these birds are missed by shooting too far in front.

Difficulty is reduced if you turn with the muzzle raised, because both the time and possible error involved in raising it and coming down again are avoided, and time is of first importance here. For consider: the bird is 'riding the punch' with all its vulnerable parts hidden, so the maximum distance at which it can be killed cleanly is about thirty-five yards.

Whether the birds be high or low your task will be very much easier if you turn quickly and with a bit of time in hand, so do not leave it to the very last moment. Turn early rather than late and, given the choice, turn to the left rather than to the right if you mount your gun on your right shoulder. You will have found out that you can get the wrong foot in front when turning to the right and, even though you must learn to shoot with your right foot forward, there is no sense in making things harder than they need be. There will be times when the mud prevents even a fair turn, but by and large you will turn as well as your boots and devotion to drill deserve. Clumsy gum-boots and bad footwork must preserve the lives of thousands of game birds every season.

15

The End of the Novice Stage

By the time the reader has reached this stage he is no longer a novice if he has followed my advice and driven each lesson home with constant practice before trying to learn the next. Certainly there is scope for improvement in the handling of his gun but he does at least know what he is trying to do, and that is a major advance. Unhappily it is seldom that we do exactly what we think we do and a looking-glass does not tell the whole story, but if you can borrow a home movie-camera you can make a big stride forward. Get a friend to make pictures of you shooting, not posing, and without you knowing whether there is a film in the camera or not. Then work on achieving a relaxed style in which your balance is kept at all times, free from all wasted movement and contorted positions but allowing plenty of adjustment in either direction without muscular constraint.

The modified stance

It will be recalled that I said that the two stances were really teaching devices and that there were so many intermediate stages that it was better to think of one stance with an infinite number of variations. At one extreme is what I have called the close stance, used when the bird is directly overhead, for then the largest fraction of the weight is on the right foot, the feet are never closer together and the left heel is never raised to a greater height. The flatter the angle at which the gun is fired, the wider apart the feet should be, with a greater part of the weight on the forward foot and the right heel tending to rise as the body is inclined forward. This reaches its limit when the target is in front of the man's feet and below their level, for then it will be seen that his body is inclined sharply forward, transferring most of the weight to the front foot while the right heel leaves the ground.

Complicating written description, though easy to execute in practice, is the fact that the weight should move towards a point vertically below the bird. You will do this correctly by instinct if you feel aggressive as you mount the gun and have a feeling that you are either driving a bayonet into the bird or putting a good straight left into its face, whether it be to the left, front or right.

A note about turning

It is fundamental that to turn to the left one should slide the left foot back in an arc and twist on the ball of the right foot, and vice versa to turn to the right, and the reader will have discovered that a turn to the right can bring his right foot in front. If there is ample time this should be corrected by moving whichever foot is carrying the least weight, but you will sometimes have to shoot with the 'wrong' foot in front.

Shooting with both eyes shut

Once a man is hitting clays thrown low down and straight away from him fairly regularly it is the custom of one famous shooting school to make him shut both eyes while he is in the process of mounting his gun. In effect he sees the clay, starts to mount, closes his eyes, completes mounting the gun and fires. More often than not he breaks the clay and the immediate lesson to be learned is that if you can hit with your eyes shut you have nothing to fear with them open, but it goes deeper than that. Surely it demonstrates both that the hands do in fact point the gun where one wants to shoot with some precision and that trained muscles will do their work without the supervision of the eyes. Golfers call this 'muscle memory' and appreciate its worth; they practise until their swing repeats itself without conscious thought, and you can do something of the same sort by constant quiet practice.

I have been ridiculed for suggesting that clays can be broken in the manner I have described, but not only have I seen it done, I have done it myself and I invite you to try. Also, if you play golf, try this: hit some shots from a peg tee with any club of medium loft before addressing the ball in the ordinary way and completing the back-

swing while looking at the ball. Then close your eyes and swing normally. The ball will probably go away just as well as the others did,
proving the real value of 'muscle memory'.

'Tromboning'

Do not make a fetish of putting the left hand at exactly the same
distance from the muzzle for every shot, but allow it to trombone
up and down the barrel comfortably. The arm must never be perfectly straight or clumsily bent, but the barrel should be allowed to
slide through the fingers during the early part of mounting and
only gripped towards the end—this is because the length of the
stock is a compromise which cannot be perfectly correct for every
shot, and the body will make its own corrections if the left hand is
allowed to slide within reason.

Shooting faster

Until the beginner has learned what he is supposed to do and does
it reasonably well it is better for him to have ample time, so I put
him where he can see the screen which protects the trap. Then he sees
the clay as early as may be. But the real difficulty of shooting game
lies in the fact that there is seldom much time available and, once
the initial difficulties have been overcome, the problem changes from
'Can I do this?' to 'Can I do it fast enough?'

This second phase of a shooting man's education is very interesting
and usually decides what final standard he will reach. It should be
remembered that the drill must never be slurred in order to gain
speed and, more important, that the best results come from starting
early and doing everything correctly the first time, without need for
alterations, rather than from moving very quickly.

The man has to shoot faster if he stands nearer the trap for oncoming birds and further from it if they are leaving him. The same
result is achieved in both cases if the clay is in flight for some time
before coming into view. No-one reaches perfection in this direction
and, no matter how good a shot a man may be, he can always learn
to shoot faster.

Strong points and weak points

I have never met a man who was equally good at all types of shot;
certainly they may be more than useful all-rounders but every one

of them is more reliable at some shot than at others and most have a weakness somewhere. For instance there are several men who are near the top of the tree at driven pheasants but who can barely hold their own against snipe. This is true of beginners as well and there are two schools of thought: Spartans make the pupil concentrate on the shots which he finds difficult, while the others keep him where he is doing well. Both are wrong, I believe, because the pupil should enjoy the lesson but leave thinking both of what he has hit and of what he has missed. Triumph and disaster should both be in his mind.

I greatly prefer to build up confidence by letting the pupil have a generous taste of what he can do well, but also to work on his weaknesses enough to raise them to a presentable standard. Confidence is a very tender plant without which none are better than sound journeymen. Certainly the essential journeyman's technique can be built up on toil alone, but even when a pupil tells me that he wants to devote an entire lesson to eliminating a particular fault, I always ensure that he has a warming-up period on something which he can do reasonably well, and ends on a note of which he can be proud. Then I show him the quiet practice I want him to do to polish his worst failings and, if he does them before he gets into his car, I know that progress has been made. That man is prepared to work but his spirit has not been broken by repeated failure.

Correcting your own mistakes

You will see the effects of hits clearly enough, so do not form the stupid habit of raising the head to see if you have hit; it is quite unnecessary and only makes shooting with the second barrel more difficult. Try, though, to make an intelligent estimate of where the shot went each time you miss. Sometimes you genuinely will not know but more often you will at least suspect that you were below, behind, over the top or something else. If there was any hesitation in the swing you probably shot behind the target, and shooting behind is a common fault. On the other hand, people with a little knowledge tend to believe that it is almost impossible to shoot too far in front, but this simply is not true. Shooting behind is indeed a common fault but most shooting men know this and many over-correct and do, in fact, shoot yards in front.

The other great cause of missing is moving the head, and if you have an impression that you saw more of the barrels than usual you probably raised your head and shot high as a consequence. But try to spot the reason for every miss without becoming a slave to theory, and try to cure your own mistakes by taking appropriate action.

Tracer cartridges can be helpful but do not be deceived by the way the tracer seems to swerve when it is near the clay; this is an optical illusion. Tracer is not really necessary once you have learned to see shot in the air but it can be reassuring.

Seeing shot in the air

The ability to see shot in the air, which all instructors have acquired and which most people can learn, is very valuable. No-one can see his own shot, because his view is obstructed by a ball of hot gases at the muzzle, and the observer should stand behind the firer's right shoulder, preferably on slightly higher ground. It is important that he should not focus his eyes on anything because what he will see is disturbed air as it comes into focus and goes out again; he should let his eyes rest idly near the clay. To me it seems that a patch of grey mist, about the size of a dinner plate, forms and lasts for less than a second.

Although a novice observer will see nothing at first, he will see the shot from at least some of them after a hundred rounds have been fired. It is difficult to see shot against a clear, blue sky but damp, overcast weather makes things easier; in mist it can often be seen plainly as a line of constant length extending at the front as it vanishes at the back.

Once two friends have learned this knack their shooting will improve very rapidly, for one can tell the other where the shot went, and it is a very short step from being told to knowing without being told, while to know where the shot went is to be a long way towards correcting the mistake. Even when most of the mistakes have been eliminated, though, and the handling of the gun is quite acceptable in the shooting field, it must be remembered that the knowledge of game takes longer to learn, and that you must still learn the ways of the shooting field.

16

Curing a Bad Patch

'I'm shooting so badly, I'd rather walk with the beaters.' Although this is often said with a cheerful grin, those with an ear for such things will usually detect a note of genuine sadness through a brave pose. We all have bad days and no matter how painstakingly we practise or how thoroughly we prepare, we cannot avoid them entirely. The best we can do is to minimize the severity of the illness.

One hallmark of a good card player is that he loses less than most people when he holds bad cards, and this is not due either to luck or to cheating, whatever the world may say. He has learned a sound technique and he sticks to it, come what may. Shooting with a shotgun is chiefly technique which practice has converted into instinctive reactions, but sometimes the conversion mechanism gets out of adjustment and the birds go flying on. The wisest course is to fall back on the basic technique and to go through the motions correctly until the birds start falling down again. The cure does not always work, but it generally does and it might work for you.

So ask your host if you may walk with the beaters, but while you do so take thought and check your grip, stance and position of the head. Insidious little errors creep in with everyone, and they may accumulate unnoticed until the shot is directed to the same, wrong place consistently. Then bring your gun up onto every leaf, twig or passing starling which catches your eye; if it does not fall into line do it again and again, secure in the knowledge that it soon will, unless you are wearing more clothes than usual.

Now imagine that thirty years have been added to your age and move as deliberately as your older self would; fix your eyes on the *head* of any bird, mount your gun on its smoke trail and swing smoothly up the trail to a long follow-through. Do this as often as you like, but when you feel more confident, press the trigger as you go past the head. The bird will probably be killed but do not worry if it is not; just swing deliberately, smoothly and bravely up the trail again, with your eyes glued to the bird's head, following through as though your life depended on it.

Deliberation is essential to accuracy and the swing must be smooth, for without smoothness the underlying mathematics are done wrongly, but if you went for the shot neither timorously nor rashly it is long odds that you hit. However, you are not quite out of the wood, and you must be very careful about the first few birds you shoot in earnest. Be quite certain that they are in range, meant to be shot and truly yours : parry doubtful calls of 'Your bird, sir' with a courteous 'No, yours, sir', because there must not be an atom of doubt in your mind as you slip into the familiar routine of mounting and swinging. Then go for the shot with a stout heart, firing at your first choice as if you had not a care in the world, and use the second barrel with unhurried calm if it is needed.

The foregoing is, of course, only a condensed refresher course of the method of shooting which I like beginners to learn; it will not always cure a loss of form but it generally does so. If there is no improvement you ought to suspect that your left eye has taken over from the right. This happens much more often than people suppose and there is nothing disgraceful about it. The scientific test is to fire at some fixed object and see if the pattern was centred far to the left. However, the alternative method of closing the left eye and seeing if the bird falls down is more practical in the shooting field.

Do not be frightened about the left eye taking over; it is highly probable that your right eye will reassert itself after a short rest, and some excellent shots habitually shoot with one eye closed. That good shooting is impossible with one eye is a fallacy—and those who say that both eyes must be used to estimate distances are invited to explain how Tommy Armour won the Open after losing the sight of an eye.

If I manage to keep my head and give this cure a fair trial it usually works; when it fails I go straight to a shooting school and put myself in their hands, secure in the knowledge that they will put me right. So far they have never failed.

There are two more things which ought to be said before we leave the subject of bad patches. First, everybody has them and feels sorry for the luckless man who is in the toils. You may feel, as I have done, that to go on making a conspicuous idiot of yourself is beyond endurance and that you will never be asked again in any case so the obvious course is to leave at once and to devote your time to gardening or anything else which can be done badly in seclusion. But you are quite wrong on a number of grounds and your spirit should be made of sterner stuff. To start with, most of the other guns have troubles enough of their own and have not even noticed what you are doing, while those who have noticed know full well that they may draw the unlucky straw next time out. Any gun who sneers knows so little of shooting that his opinion cannot be of consequence.

Second, you have the task of not allowing your misery to overflow and spoil the day for other people. By all means express regret to your host for doing less than justice to his birds but never make excuses, bewail your fate or look glum.

An old keeper, my friend from childhood, may have reached the heart of this chapter when he came upon me disconsolate beside a large number of fired cartridges and a negligible addition to the bag. He told me firmly to 'Let that gun swing freely, like you generally do. I'll see that you're asked next time.' I swung as freely as panic permitted and I think that I was back to normal by the time the next drive ended.

17

Advanced Shooting

The first step towards advanced shooting, by which I mean employing effective but unorthodox methods, is to learn to shoot from cramped or difficult positions. It is often necessary to fire when sitting in a hide or with one's feet stuck deep in mud and the important thing is to be able to improvise. With practice a longish swing can be made by relaxing the hips and waist, and certainly this is better than relying on the arms and a twist of the spine alone, but it is better still to move everything which can be swung. The lower down the swing starts the greater the angle through which the gun can be swung without constraint, and even if your feet are stuck tight you can get a bit of give from your ankles, more still from your knees and so on. That is about as far as advice is helpful—for the rest it is best to follow one's natural bent; I would rather shoot kneeling on one knee than sitting and have no great objection to lying flat on my back on the side of an embankment, but others prefer different improvisations.

Shortening the swing

It would be wrong to suggest that shooting is easy even when all the time one wants is available but it is much harder when there is little time to spare, and one of the foundations of quicker shooting is the fact that trained hands put the gun on the target long before the butt reaches the shoulder. To convince the reader that this is true of him I invite him to fire a few shots with the butt clamped between the upper arm and the side and with his eyes glued to the target, much as in the ready position. There is nothing against starting with stationary targets, and tracer cartridges can be helpful, but the chances

64

are that he will hit some oncoming clays thrown to represent driven partridges. Of course the recoil must be respected, and a small-bore gun can be used if doubt exists, but anyone who learned to fire the ·303 service rifle from the hip can use a 12-bore without a qualm.

Once convinced that the hands really do put the gun on when held in this manner, you can use the method undiluted if you wish, for I have seen snipe shot in this way, but I have yet to meet a single man who under pressure did not prefer if possible to shoot while in the process of mounting the gun. In fact moving pictures show that many men fire before the butt is on the shoulder without realizing that they have done so. It should not be done deliberately except when pressed for time, and it is only a shortened version of the fundamental method, but sceptics should not brush it aside as fanciful, for it has stood the test of time.

As one sees a rabbit dashing for its burrow one may realize that it will be out of sight in less time than normal mounting and firing requires, but training ensures that mounting and swinging start together sub-consciously and one just fires *whether the butt has reached the shoulder or not*, gambling on the fact that the hands put the gun on very early in the process of mounting. The same circumstances often arise with snipe, but in this case it is difficult to make a film of the shot and to convince the man that he really fired before the butt reached his shoulder. It is easy, however, to film a hot corner at driven game and then it can be seen that, although the gun is almost always swung, it is often fired when far from the shoulder if the angle is flat and without quite reaching the shoulder when the angle is steep.

The lesson to be learned is that with a proper grip and stance, together with a swing which starts as mounting begins, we can all learn to kill game without completing the mounting of the gun, but the kick must never be disdained, for the first hint of disrespect will be avenged with ferocity.

It is in shooting of this kind that the handling qualities of the gun show their worth; a clumsy and poorly-fitted gun will serve when the man has time to think, but when the brain must give way to reflex action, results depend mainly on the fit and handling qualities.

Intercepting birds

However much the swing is contracted, and it should be noticed that the whole of the foregoing refers to shooting while the gun is

E

swinging, it is quite another matter to attempt to intercept a bird in flight with the gun stationary. This *is* possible, and it is fun to try it now and again, but it does not really pay a dividend. It may be that you see a woodcock flickering among the trees and decide to intercept it as it crosses the only space clear enough to give you even the ghost of a chance; if you see enough flickers to pick up the 'cock's track in your mind before it reaches the clear space you may bring off a shot which you will remember, but the chances of a kill are small.

Automatic allowance

Figure 8 shows the theory which applies, of course, only to oncoming shots. Some experts raise their heads just the right amount and swing so that the bird rides along the muzzle to certain death, but the whole brittle structure collapses when the tiniest error creeps in. When this method is working well it is probably the most effective which exists, but unless it is in perfect adjustment it does not work at all. I suspect, only suspect, that the wonderfully long series of

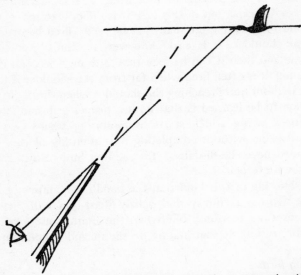

Figure 8. Automatic allowance. This is used only at oncoming birds. If the eye is raised just the correct amount, the bird is seen over the muzzle when the barrels point the proper amount ahead of the bird.

consecutive kills, with the man picking his birds and killing them all at about the same place in the sky, were made with the aid of automatic allowance. Experts know when to use it but the ordinary performer should treat the method as a dangerous acquaintance, because the by-product may be that he raises his head unconsciously; then he can hit nothing until he has re-formed the habit of moving his head to the proper place and keeping it there.

Some instructors prefer their pupils to have nothing to do with either intercepting or automatic allowance. Most of us certainly would get better results by sticking to the basic methods, but shooting is more enjoyable if one sometimes stretches up for prizes which are really out of reach. I am a poor Bridge player, but I like to study the wonderful end-plays and squeezes which famous players produce; I cannot do them properly in play, and the probability is that they are beyond me, but I enjoy Bridge more if I strive occasionally for the higher standard. The same applies to shooting. For the bulk of the time it is wise to remember one's limitations and to keep within them, but one should also have some knowledge of the higher levels and take a step in their direction now and then.

The moving dot

This is something about which I write with diffidence because, although I do it myself when at the top of my form, I am not quite certain what I do. The scheme is to think of a dot moving along in front of the bird and just shoot at it. Films shows that my gun is swung, but they are neither smoke trail nor Churchill swings, and whether a bit of forward allowance or flair creeps in I honestly do not know.

18

Something of the Hidden Mathematics

Please do not shy away from the word mathematics like a startled colt; however intensely you hated the subject at school, even if arithmetic was a grinding toil and algebra an incomprehensible waste of time, all the maths we need can be turned into interesting reading for those with a taste for such problems and, for readers who cannot stand the prospect of doing sums, the conclusions are put first so that they can see the essentials without wading through the calculations.

I confess that I find mathematical problems interesting, although I avoid the crosswords and chess problems which fascinate some people, but my real reason for introducing the subject is to show some of the half-truths and false analogies which surround shooting in their true light and to demonstrate that forward allowance has serious shortcomings in practice.

If the target was struck by the centre of the pattern it cannot be denied that the gun was fired in the right direction; and reflection shows that there is only one such direction no matter what method the firer used to find it. Later in the chapter I shall calculate where this one correct point is for a number of typical shots and show what data must be available to the firer if he uses four well-known methods to direct his gun at that spot.

Some of the facts which the following calculations will show to be true beyond dispute are:

1. An allowance of 6 feet 8 inches is necessary for a very common shot, and those people who genuinely believe that they ever hit such

a bird by shooting straight at it are genuinely mistaken. They must be among those who do not do what they think they do.

2. A man who uses the smoke trail method must swing at the correct speed but needs no data concerning range, speed, course, wind or anything else. He has one unknown quantity only.

3. One who uses the Churchill swing must fire at the correct instant after speeding up the swing by the correct amount, but he needs no other data. Thus he has two unknown quantities.

4. A forward allowance man who swings an estimated *linear distance* ahead of the bird must know the range, the speed of the bird and its course relative to himself, the speed and direction of the wind and whether the bird be climbing, diving or in horizontal flight. This is a total of six unknowns.

5. A forward allowancer who swings an estimated *angle* ahead of the bird needs all this data except the range. So he must cope with five unknowns.

6. The effect of the wind upon a bird in flight is very significant; quite a normal breeze can double, or halve, the allowance required in still air and, just as important, the wind pushes a bird sideways.

It is self-evident that any estimate may be inaccurate, so a method which requires no estimates is inherently sounder unless it calls for a degree of manual dexterity even more liable to error. Applying this principle to shooting technique, the difference in degree of manual skill required is the decisive point when choosing between the Churchill and smoke trail methods.

In forward allowance it is better to estimate an angle than a linear distance, but it is quite impossible for any man to make all the estimates and do the calculations in the time available. The best that can be done in the shooting field is to memorize the angles for a number of typical shots, and to add or subtract a bit as judgment says is proper. If we had radar to gather the data and calculating machines to do the sums forward allowance might be deadly, but until that time comes let us recognize forward allowance for what it is—an approximation which works quite often.

It is perfectly reasonable to ask how it can be possible that the Churchill and smoke trail methods call for no data or calculations to reach the same point which I locate below only after doing long sums on paper. I distrust analogies but I am going to use one now. If your life depended upon knowing the square root of 17·3 multiplied by 3·9 you could slog it out on paper, but logarithms would make things easier and a slide rule would give the answer in a fraction of the time. Even if you had no idea of the theory of slide rules you would find the correct answer quickly. The point is that there are easy ways of doing difficult sums and, if you know the ropes, you can solve intricate problems without using figures at all or having one single clue as to how it is done. Even if you go through a routine without comprehension the answer will manifest itself.

Graphical methods are one of the standard routines for avoiding laborious calculations and it is long odds that every girder bridge you cross and every roof with a steel truss beneath which you shelter was worked out by a simple graphical method. The man who drew the diagrams was probably a sound mathematician but they *can* be drawn by a man who can barely count. When you swing a gun on a moving bird, unknown to yourself, you are solving a most complex problem by a graphical method. The muzzle takes account of every single factor with precision: whether the bird be fast or slow, climbing or diving, aided by the wind, pushed sideways or anything else, the muzzle absorbs all the facts and works out the bird's course and speed relative to you—which is what you want to know. In the jargon of mathematics the muzzle travels down the 'resultant' when it swings on; when it is swung ahead of the bird it is predicting its future position by extending that resultant. All the data has been gathered and the calculations have been made, but graphical methods have taken the place of figures and that the lines have been drawn by the muzzle in the air instead of by a pencil upon paper is not significant.

The calculations

Let us assume that:

1.   The target moves at 60 feet per second (40·9 mph), which is about the speed of a pheasant in still air.

2.   That the shot has a constant velocity of 1,080 feet per second at all sporting ranges, although we know that it slows down slightly in flight.

3.   That the gun is always fired due north unless the context indicates otherwise.

THE CROSSING SHOT: Consider a bird crossing at eye level from east to west 40 yards out. While the shot goes 40 yards (120 feet) at

1,080 feet per second the bird will travel the correct forward allowance (F A) at 60 fps, so the correct F A is 120 divided by $\frac{1,080}{60}$ which is 6·66 feet. Similarly the F A at 30 yards is 4·995 feet and at 20 yards is 3·33 feet. Notice that the angular allowance is the same in every case: its tangent is $\frac{6·66}{120}$ or $\frac{4·995}{90}$ or $\frac{3·33}{60}$, which is 0·0555 every time. Tangent tables show that this angle is 3 degrees and 11 minutes approximately.

WIND HELPING OR HINDERING THE BIRD: Inspection shows that for each 10·2 mph of wind helping or hindering the bird 25% should be added to or subtracted from the above allowances, and this is important because 25% of 6·66 feet is 20 inches and greater than the radius of the accepted killing circle at 40 yards. So if you shoot accurately but make no allowance for wind you will miss a small target every time there is a head or tail wind of 10·2 mph or more.

ONCOMING BIRDS WHEN THE GUN IS FIRED VERTICALLY UPWARDS: Notice that the allowances for oncoming birds when the gun is fired vertically upwards are the same as those for crossing birds at eye level.

QUARTERING SHOTS: If a bird is coming from the north-east and will cross your front 40 yards out, with you shooting due north, it will still travel 6·66 feet while the shot goes 40 yards but, due to foreshortening, this will appear to be less. It is the apparent allowance which the shooter wants to know, and from the north-east it is just two-thirds of that needed for a plain crossing shot.

Figure 9 shows how this is worked out, and oncoming birds require the same amount if the gun is fired at an elevation of forty-five degrees above the horizontal. Notice, however, that each different angle of approach calls for a different calculation using the same method; half the angle does not mean half the allowance because the tangent of the angle, not simple arithmetic, controls things.

THE EFFECT OF A SIDE WIND: If a bird's own efforts propel it southwards at sixty feet per second while a north-easterly wind blows at thirty feet per second its course and speed over the ground can be found by trigonometry, but I will use a graphical method because that is how the muzzle does it. Just plot the velocities and directions to scale, as in Figure 10, complete the parallelogram and the diagonal will lie in the direction of the bird's path while the length of the

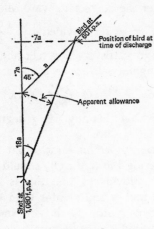

Figure 9

Tan A = ·7a / 18·7a = ·0374. Therefore A is 2 degrees and 8 minutes
approximately, which is two-thirds
of the angular allowance for a bird
coming from the east.

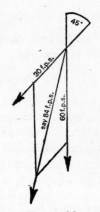

Figure 10
The effect of a side wind.

diagonal gives its speed to scale. The diagonal is called the 'resultant', and the muzzle of a gun swung on traces it exactly; that the speed of the swing, as distinct from the length of the line on paper, gives the speed of the bird does not alter the underlying theory.

The muzzle looks after all the problems of fore-shortening and changes of height in much the same way and all at the same time without the man necessarily knowing anything about them. If we knew that a quartering bird was climbing at such and such an angle we could do some more calculations and combine the results to reach a grand total; but a gun swung on will give exactly the same result as the profoundest mathematics without the need for estimates or the ability to count, let alone calculate.

THE NEED FOR A SMOOTH SWING: It will be recalled that I frequently emphasized that the swing up the smoke trail must be smooth and it will now be clear that if this is not so the muzzle will give the wrong answer concerning speed.

Final thoughts about the calculations

Most certainly the one spot at which we all wish to shoot can be located by mathematics; indeed, sophisticated anti-aircraft guns shot down flying bombs by the hundred using even more complicated methods, for they intercepted with stationary guns. However, I have shown that it is quite impossible to gather the necessary data in the shooting field or to complete the calculations in the time available, even if on the face of it any system which is founded on sound mathematics should be more accurate unless it has some built-in weakness which more than counterbalances its inherent strength.

It is hard to make out a logical case in favour of forward allowance yet many people use it with success. Presumably these men have brought their judgment to such a pitch that it triumphs over the fundamental flaws, and it would be very interesting to know how much better or worse they would shoot if they made a whole-hearted attempt to learn one of the swinging methods.

19

Which is the Best Method?

We humans vary so much that there is certainly no one method which is best suited to everyone; each system will yield the best results to somebody. To misquote Kipling, 'There are nine and sixty ways of constructing tribal lays, and every single one of them is right for someone.' It is equally certain that each of us is likely to make the wisest choice for himself if the problem is approached with a receptive mind and the advantages and limitations of each method are examined in the cold light of reason. Habit, prejudice and mental inertia are powerful forces but they should be banished from the mind if the factors are to be weighed fairly so that the wisest conclusion can be reached.

It is in this spirit that I say that if a man has a clumsy gun which is grossly ill-fitting he has no choice but to aim it as he would a rifle, and to use one of the two variations of forward allowance. Even so, he will do better if he makes an angular allowance rather than one of linear distance, for this eliminates the need for an accurate estimate of the range. It is therefore inherently more accurate and should always be used provided that the man can judge angles. If he sticks to linear distances he has a permanent handicap.

By the same token, both the smoke trail and the Churchill swings have built-in advantages since they require no estimates whatever, but they do call for guns which are reasonably well-fitted and for greater manual dexterity. Here we have to cope with one of the great obstacles to clear thinking, the half-truth which has been repeated so often that it is accepted as true beyond question. In this case the half-truth takes some form akin to 'My dear sir, a good shot can shoot well with any gun.' Having seen excellent shots take my own gun from me and break difficult clays with it to demonstrate some point, I know that there is an element of truth in this, as my gun has a stock an inch too long for some of the demonstrators. But, having talked to the demonstrators, I also know that it is not completely true. They had enough skill to alter their grip sufficiently to cancel the misfit yet still break the clay. However, if they had to shoot for their lives, which is another way of saying if they wished to reach their full potential, each and every one of them would remove the handicap of an imperfect grip and use a well-fitted gun.

Assuming that a well-fitted gun is used a balance can be struck between the smoke trail swing and that described by Churchill. My own experience is that the smoke trail method is easier both to teach and to learn, but it does not follow that it is necessarily superior for all time. Once a novice has gained enough dexterity he may do better with Churchill's method and he should make the trial.

I start every big day as a smoke trailer, slide happily into Churchill as I warm up and, if things go extra well, probably end the day by snapping at an imaginary dot moving along ahead of the birds. If things go wrong at any stage I go straight back to the smoke trail, because that calls for a degree of skill which I can usually muster. Some men may be so skilled that they can start with an advanced method, but I think that a warming-up period on something known to be reliable benefits most of us. Churchill's swing probably calls for more manual skill, more dexterity, but if a man has that skill he will get closer to his full potential by switching to Churchill. However, it calls for some extra talent and a lot of recent practice to make Churchill's method profitable and many men do better by sticking to the smoke trail. This is no criticism of Churchill, far from it: he was a man of outstanding talent who shot game or clays on something like three hundred days every year, but what such a man can do as a matter of routine with perfectly fitted guns may be beyond the powers of less talented men shooting much less frequently.

Because I do not assert that the smoke trail method, which I named but did not originate, is the best for all men in all circumstances it has been alleged that I am spineless, infirm of purpose and incapable of making up my mind. I am apparently expected to uphold its overwhelming merit to the death against all comers even though reason tells me that it would be foolish to make such a claim. It is best to start a novice on the smoke trail, and he must stick to one method until he has mastered it, because he falls irretrievably between the stools if he does not; once he has reached a standard equivalent to that of a middle handicap golfer he should be flexible. Surely the ideal would be to have such a mastery of all the methods that we adopted the one best suited to the shot in hand without conscious thought, and I say that it should be without thought advisedly because if you have a change of heart after your first movement you will probably produce a mongrel effort and a poor shot.

Part Two

Guns, Equipment Etc

20

The Cost and Ways of Taking Up Shooting

Let the cost of taking up shooting deter no man for many, many a novice has embarked upon an occupation which has given lifelong pleasure by purchasing one box of cartridges, of which the present (1972) price is a little over £1·00. (*NB.* all prices in this chapter are 1972 prices.) With these, a borrowed gun and the permission of a friendly farmer he had all he needed for enjoyment. Nowadays he must obtain a shotgun certificate from the police (25p) and he should insure against accident although this is not compulsory. Insurance costs about £1·50 a year.

The first additional piece of equipment is always a piece of string with which to tie together the necks of birds so that they can be carried in comfort, and every other item is accumulated over the years as opportunity offers.

Shooting, like so many things, costs as much or as little as one cares to spend upon it. A new double-barrelled 12-bore costs anything from about £53 to over £1,500 plus purchase tax and one buys a gun one can afford. Similarly with clothes: a perfectly adequate shooting suit can be made from one of your older tweed suits by the village tailor and you will shoot just as well in it as in one from Savile Row. Pigskin cartridge bags, leather gun cases and elaborate shooting sticks are very nice, the good ones are a joy to own, but they are not essential and most people only purchase those which do not arrive as presents.

Lessons at a good school, each of one hour and using up to one hundred cartridges and clays, cost about £15 each at 1972 prices. If he can afford six lessons no beginner could make a better investment; more are probably unnecessary if he really does his quiet practice but many a determined man has reached a high standard with fewer, or indeed with none at all. Many people who take shooting seriously like to have two or three lessons to get into form before the season begins; it is an enormous advantage to do so but it is not essential and it raises the shooting man's perpetual dilemma of 'Should I spend the £X which I can spare on equipment, on lessons or on something to shoot at?' Some of the happiest day-dreams revolve about this problem.

Almost the only shooting which can be obtained for the cost of cartridges alone is at pigeon or wildfowl though invitations to shoot do tend to find their way to really good performers. Some idea of the cost of various kinds of shooting can be found in chapter 28, but there is no need to despair if ambition out-ranges the purse because you can rent a piece of land and have a fascinating time building up a shoot as a do-it-yourself gamekeeper. For people who like it there is no better hobby but it is outside the scope of this book. Rents vary widely throughout the country but in my part of southern England unkeepered land lets at about 25p per acre per year and keepered land for almost double that.

You will both see and retrieve much more game if you have a dog. Either a springer or a labrador costs between £55 and £90 a year to keep; some people pay £200 or more for a trained gun-dog while others cadge a puppy, train it themselves and get much the same result.

If I were taking up shooting with unlimited funds at my disposal I should buy the best clothes, boots and ancillary equipment from the outset, and I should take pains to dull its brilliance by use in private for it should all look slightly worn, but I should not order a pair of 'best' guns from a top notch London maker until experience had trained my palate, as it were. Such guns are the best in the world, they are the rare vintages, the Classic winners and the Rolls-Royces of their own sphere, but an honest boxlock is far more suitable for a beginner. It has a toughness, a hardihood, which can resist the rough handling to which every novice exposes his gun. From all but the cheapest boxlocks a man will obtain eighty years or more of excellent service and let it be clearly understood that a boxlock costing about

£500 including purchase tax (1972 price) is a far better gun than most of us will ever be shots. They lack some of the refinements of 'best' guns but their shooting performance is no more than a hair's breadth behind. A cynic might say that this figure is £100 too high but as we have no reliable yardstick for measuring the qualities of guns or the performance of shooters let us not indulge in discussion which cannot be conclusive.

When a man has learned enough to discriminate let him have first-class guns made to measure by all means; they are much nicer to use but he will not necessarily shoot better with them. It is not true to say that skill is always the decisive factor, for the best of shots cannot even hold his own unless his gun is up to a certain standard, but every season one sees skilled men out-shooting the field with boxlocks which only the most charitable would describe as honest. Nevertheless if other things are equal a 'best' will tip the scale and it is always a source of great pleasure to those who can appreciate superlative craftsmanship.

The following list of famous names reads like a wine list in that the relative merits can be debated at length and weighed against the costs:

A.Y.A. Guns, A.S.I., Alliance House, Snape, Saxmundham, Suffolk.

T. Bland & Sons Ltd, 4 & 5 William IV Street, West Strand, London, W.C.2.

Boss & Co. Ltd, 13–14 Cork Street, London, W.1.

Churchill, Atkin, Grant & Lang Ltd, 7 Bury Street, St James, London, S.W.1.

Cogswell & Harrison Ltd, 168 Piccadilly, London, S.W.1.

John Dickson and Son, 21 Frederick Street, Edinburgh.

W. W. Greener Ltd, see under Webley & Scott Ltd.

Holland & Holland Ltd, 13 Bruton Street, London, W.1.

W. J. Jeffery & Co. Ltd, once of Golden Square. See under Holland & Holland.

James Purdey & Sons Ltd, 57–58 South Audley Street, London, W.1.

Webley & Scott Ltd, Park Lane, Handsworth, Birmingham.

Westley Richards & Co. Ltd, Grange Road, Birmingham. The London Agency is now at Holland & Holland's.

Although these firms cover a great range nothing short of a trade directory could list all the well known gun makers of this country alone while some good guns are made in Spain, Germany, Austria and Italy. The shortness of the list reflects only the limitations of space and casts no slur on the many renowned names which are omitted with regret. It is sad to record that one of the most worthy of the honest workhorses, the B.S.A. gun, is no longer made.

Every gun maker, and almost every gun shop, has links with a shooting school while others can be located by studying the advertisements in the *Shooting Times*.

So much for the tangible problems, none of which are difficult to solve if taken one at a time, but there is one which may bring defeat by undermining the resolution. This springs from the undoubted fact that for much of the year many of us go to work and return home in the dark so that we only see our wives in daylight at the weekends. If shooting causes separation on Saturdays as well it may be opposed so the wise man suggests that both should learn together. Women can shoot every bit as well as men and no great muscular development is called for. In less guarded terms she does not have to be a hockey type to shoot well. Learning with someone else is far more interesting, far easier and much, much cheaper.

It is often noticed that a woman who consents to try her hand at shooting either drops the idea after the briefest acquaintance or becomes an enthusiast and learns very quickly. Her rapid progress often outstrips that of a male pupil largely because she comes to the problems with no preconceived ideas but accepts instruction without question. Very few men have neither played with airguns nor have used firearms in earnest before their first serious lesson with a shotgun and they are seldom prepared to trust an instructor implicitly from the outset.

21

Choosing a Gun for Game

Shooting men vary so much in their tastes and the purposes to which they put their guns that some gun, be it a 28-bore automatic or a single-barrelled 4-bore, will be someone's favourite. At first sight the vast number of the alternative choices may be bewildering but things will become clearer as soon as it is realized that no one gun is ideal for all purposes, even for one man, and that every gun is a compromise between those eternal enemies power, weight, handling qualities and recoil.

If the power is increased the gun must be more strongly constructed so, normally, the weight will be increased and the handling qualities will be diminished thereby. If, by using special materials and designs, a very light gun of great power were produced it might handle to perfection but the recoil would be more than most of us could endure. It is, of course, possible to propel a stated load of shot at a stated velocity from barrels of quite different bores, but experience has shown that, by and large, a 12-bore has the best proportions for our purpose.

If there were a standard game gun in this country, which there is not, it would probably be a double-barrelled 12-bore chambered for 2½-inch cartridges because this is a compromise which is satisfactory to many people for shooting game. It is much less suitable for breaking clays so different guns have been developed for clay shooting specialists; these are well adapted to their own purpose but not to those of the game shot.

So let us think of the 2½-inch 12-bore as the middle of the scale and work outwards considering the alternatives. On the more power-

ful side there is, first, the 2¾-inch 12-bore giving a shade more power
but demanding a slightly better physique from its handler. Next
comes the 3-inch 12-bore, heavier and more powerful still, which has
largely replaced the 10- and 8-bores beloved by wildfowlers of former
times. Some of these big bores are still in use but they are specialized
weapons whose popularity is fading, partly because their cartridges
are very expensive.

First on the lighter side of the average is a choice between the
2-inch 12-bore and the 2½-inch 16-bore. These guns are equal bewteen
themselves and they are often preferred by ladies, lightweights and
men past their physical best. They are perfectly adequate against
most driven game and they are only at a disadvantage of any significance when the ranges lengthen. The 2¾-inch 16-bore is so like
the 2½-inch 12-bore that personal taste alone can make the
choice.

To get the same performance from a 20-bore throwing no more
than ¾ of an ounce of shot calls for considerably more skill but it
is a deadly weapon in skilled hands. Some ladies prefer it to all others,
it is excellent for beginners and is a safe refuge from gun-headaches.
Unfortunately as soon as one attempts to increase the power of a
20-bore one is liable to produce a gun which kicks viciously. Although
28-bores find favour because they are very light I think that they
demand more skill than is given to most of us, but there are seldom
two opinions about a ·410: it is a boy's gun and ideal for the
purpose.

This is a good place to make the point that the purpose for which
a gun will be chiefly used is of importance. If most of a man's shooting is at driven partridges he would be wise to favour handling
qualities at the expense of power but to reverse his preference if the
bulk of his shooting were, say, to be at flighting duck. By the same
token he will be prepared to accept more recoil, and reap the advantages of lightness, if he only fires a few shots than if he habitually
uses many cartridges in a day.

Without much doubt the best results are obtained by bringing a
relatively low-powered gun into action quickly and accurately, but
over-emphasis should be avoided because there is no sense in sacrificing power in order to gain more speed than is necessary in practice.
The man who can *genuinely* handle a more powerful gun fast enough
for the task in hand always has an advantage. What is utterly wrong,

and it is a very common mistake, is to attempt to make good a suspected lack of skill by using a more powerful gun or cartridge. Far
from helping the unskilful this only makes things more difficult.

Factors which affect the selection of any gun

Whatever bore and length of cartridge is selected some features
are common to all game guns. For reasons which may or may not
be valid, neither pump guns nor automatics are popular among game
shots in this country. I myself find that their handling qualities are
different and that I shoot badly with them but there are other objec-
tions (see page 129) and, for the time being at any rate, their use in
formal game shooting should not be considered. For all serious game
shooting double-barrelled guns are used, with side-by-sides far out-
numbering over-and-unders.

The most expensive guns are always double-barrelled hammerless
ejectors and the more a gun departs from that description the cheaper
it should be if other things are equal. A non-ejector is cheaper but
slower to reload, while a hammer gun is cheaper still, even slower
to bring into action and inherently more dangerous. It might be
thought that the simpler actions would be more reliable, since there
is less to go wrong, but good hammerless ejectors 'never' break down
if they are looked after properly, and this applies to boxlocks as well
as to sidelocks. The history of the development of guns has caused
sidelocks to be more highly regarded than boxlocks, and this was
justified long ago, but there is really very little to choose between
them nowadays, and I should always prefer a good boxlock to a
second-rate sidelock.

Single triggers should be selective unless both barrels have the same
degree of choke, and not everyone likes them. At present no single-
trigger mechanism is as reliable as a two-triggered mechanism, nor
is the rate of fire increased. There may be some advantage in that
the identical grip is used for both barrels, but that a glove can be
used on the right hand and that bruising on the trigger guard is
avoided seem to be side issues.

Detachable locks and all the devices for easy opening and closing
are neither gimmicks nor essentials; when they function perfectly
they add to excellence but if they break down not one word can be
said in their favour.

The vexed problem of the right degree of choke is also common to all bores and a gun used for general purposes will be about right with half-choke in the left barrel and improved cylinder in the right. Those concentrating on driven game might do better with a little less choke though wildfowlers might prefer a trifle more. The most suitable chokes can be debated at length but where doubt exists the fuller choke should always be selected because it can easily be reduced but it can never be increased.

Guns made from soft metal wear out quickly no matter how well they are looked after and those with parts 'fitted' under stress are unreliable because repeated firing relieves the internal stress in the metal and the parts no longer fit. Though such guns can be bought new for small sums their short lives make them the most expensive of all.

Finally every gun must be in proof at the time of purchase, but proof and proof marks are such a complicated and vital matter that a separate chapter is devoted to them.

The length of the barrels of 12-bore guns

The choice of the length of the barrels confuses the issue to such an extent that these notes are confined to 12-bore guns where the lengths range from twenty-five inches to thirty; anything longer than thirty inches is obsolete. Without wishing to revive the controversy which arose when Churchill introduced the XXV gun it is a matter of fact that his guns with twenty-five-inch barrels weigh about half a pound less than their opposite numbers with longer barrels; they handle very fast and give the shot a slightly lower velocity, although this has no significance in practice. However, it is fairly certain that they do not suit everybody and they are probably seen at their best in the hands of short, thickset men of placid temperament; others seem to do better with longer barrels, possibly because a trifle more deliberation is enforced. The very short barrels certainly come 'on' very quickly but sometimes they come 'off' again.

Barrels thirty inches long are perfectly sound but a trifle old-fashioned; twenty-eight inches is probably the most popular length with twenty-seven inches in second place, while twenty-six inches is suspect on the same grounds as twenty-five inches.

It must not be thought, however, that every gun with twenty-five-inch barrels will handle well. Good handling stems from a subtle combination of weight and balance and though short barrels bring fast handling within a designer's reach the opportunity may not be grasped.

Establishing a short list of the candidates

At this point the rational step is to select the type of gun best suited to the purpose in mind and then to find a gun of that type whose price is within one's means. Any other approach is liable to result in the purchase of a gun which is wonderful value for money but useless for shooting the game available.

In spite of the vast number of permutations possible a fairly clear picture of the best gun for any particular case will emerge if the problem is stated clearly and honestly. Thus many men of average strength and size who needed one gun to serve for walking-up, some driving and some pigeon and wildfowl shooting would be wise to choose a double-barrelled side-by-side 2½-inch 12-bore weighing between 6 lb 6 oz and 6 lb 10 oz. The barrels should be twenty-eight inches long with half-choke in the left barrel and improved cylinder in the right. It is better, though not essential, to decide at this time whether the gun is to have one trigger or two but the fact that it will be used against driven game makes the choice of a hammerless ejector almost automatic.

Similar guns chambered for 2¾-inch cartridges are justly popular but they weigh a little more; if a lighter gun is desired either a 2-inch 12-bore or a 2½-inch 16 is admirable.

The guns described above would be sensibly chosen for the purposes stated, but a rational case can certainly be made for a 12-bore chambered for 2¾-inch cases with barrels twenty-five inches long. That there are several correct solutions to the same problem only adds to the interest.

The price of a gun

Once the type of gun to be bought has been decided it is not difficult to match one's purse to the type because all types of guns are made in three, or perhaps four, different price ranges. Broadly speaking the prices reflect the gun's 'quality' in the sense in which the word is used of a horse, and my own three guns are a good example of how this works in practice.

They are all 12-bore, double-barrelled hammerless ejectors and they all kill game equally well if fired in the right direction. The minor differences in their patterns and ballistics are much less than the shooting errors of ordinary mortals and they have all lasted well and have proved to be utterly reliable, yet their purchase prices and their present day values are poles apart. My 'lending' gun cost eighteen guineas when new in 1934; it is tough and hardy, but although it was altered to fit me I find that it is too cumbersome and heavy for me to shoot well with it. My 'best' gun cost sixty pounds when new in 1909 and its present value makes me respect it as a long-term investment. Its famous maker altered it to fit me when I inherited it. My 'second' gun, from the same famous maker, cost thirty pounds when new in 1908; I bought it from the maker for sixty-five pounds in 1948 and it is worth very much more now.

It will be noticed that the 'best' cost twice as much as the 'second' and there is a good reason for this, even though the fit and handling qualities are almost equal and both are reliable and long-lived. A 'best' by a top-grade maker has nothing but the best materials, design and workmanship; the cost is not considered and it is beyond question that this combination produces the finest result, but this last bit of excellence is very hard to come by and adds greatly to the cost. Something of the same sort is seen if a good watch is compared with a chronometer, but a more vivid comparison is that between the winners of the Derby and the Grand National. The one is only some 5 mph faster than the other yet to obtain that small increase of speed it is necessary to remove three stones of weight, thirty fences and to reduce the distance from $4\frac{1}{2}$ miles to $1\frac{1}{2}$.

'Second' guns made by good makers, and those made by firms which do not attempt to enter the top price market, often have a lot of quality and they are made, or altered, to suit each customer. They are the result of an attempt to strike a rational balance between cost, quality and the tastes of the buyers and it would be foolish to under-rate them. Good design, first-class materials and wonderful craftsmanship are not peculiar to best guns; they have them in full measure but most certainly not to the exclusion of all others.

Some reputable manufacturers employ modern techniques to produce guns which all leave the factory with full choke in both barrels and standard woodwork but they are not sold off the peg. The chokes and woodwork are altered to suit each customer so that there is a large bespoke element together with the lowering of costs expected from large-scale production.

My own relations with the gun trade have been of the happiest, although the fact that I have made it a rule to deal only with firms which really valued their reputations may have had something to do with this. Such firms will guide a layman and he can easily find out the prices of new guns of different grades. Any new gun bought from a firm of good repute is worth just about the price paid for it.

Second-hand guns

There has always been a big market in second-hand guns and this may well be the place to find the best value for money, but the purchaser should be alert. Fashion affects the price, and although famous makers are always in fashion the taste for short barrels, single triggers and sidelocks is relatively new. If there be bargains in second-hand guns they will probably be found with thirty-inch barrels, boxlocks and two triggers.

I sometimes wonder if all the facts are volunteered, even by the most reputable establishments, unless such questions as 'Are these the original barrels?' are asked, but I have never been given an untruthful answer to a direct question. Even so I greatly prefer to buy a used gun from the maker and, were I contemplating a purchase from another source, I should have the gun vetted by the maker.

Let us consider this briefly: a famous name on the rib is no guarantee that inferior barrels were not substituted; the maker will detect this but a layman may not. Even if all the parts are genuine the wear may be such that a little more shooting will put the gun out of proof or, a deadly pitfall, what appears to be a 'second' which has seen hardship may, in fact, be of the 'lending' grade. A reputable maker will steer a prospective buyer of his guns away from disaster.

Surely the fair price for a gun bought from a friend is half-way between the buying and selling prices after the maker has vetted it.

There are special auctions where the organizers are well-informed on matters pertaining to guns, but at the ordinary sale of goods no-one without special skills and measuring instruments can bid with safety. The gun may be what it appears, perhaps a best in mint condition, but it may be on the brink of failing a proof test.

How much then should be paid for a gun? I pay as much as I can afford and care for the gun meticulously. Then I have a good quality gun all my life at much less cost than that of a series of second-raters. The exception is my 'lending' gun, which satisfies me as long as it is safe and reliable.

Barrels which print their patterns in different places

It may be true that for certain specialized forms of shooting it can be an advantage to have barrels which centre their patterns in different places, but but for ordinary, mixed game shooting it is a serious disadvantage. The whole purpose of a well-fitted gun is defeated if one barrel shoots where the man intends but the other directs its load somewhere else. Those whose line of thought runs 'The common fault being such and such, a barrel which anticipates this fault and corrects it is beneficial' are building on defective foundations. How in the world do they know that the future purchaser of one particular gun will make the common error? The divergence of one barrel may add to his habitual mistake instead of correcting it. Secondly, men can be educated and it is better that they should correct their own faults rather than that they should rely upon an eccentric gun to do it for them, for it must never be forgotten that a divergent barrel which corrects one fault automatically introduces another.

To expand on this: let us imagine that the left barrel shoots where the man intends but that the right shoots appreciably higher and that this is supposed to eliminate the common fault of shooting behind high oncoming birds. This might be so, but the right barrel will infallibly shoot over the top of low crossing birds unless the man makes a deliberate effort to shoot low with it. Surely the gun should be correctly regulated and the man should learn to use it properly? However, I should like to emphasize that I am referring to the regulation which ensures that both barrels centre their patterns in the same place, not to altering the stock to suit an idividual.

Single-barrelled guns

These are best considered by themselves because they are usually used for rather different purposes. Some good quality single-barrelled guns have been made, but they are rare; those commonly seen are intended to satisfy the perfectly legitimate demand for a cheap, handy gun which can be used without a qualm in rough conditions.

At first sight one would expect them to be the cheapest, lightest and quickest to bring into action but, while this is probably true on all counts, it is by a smaller margin than might be expected. It is not much more expensive to make a double-barrelled gun once the tools and skill are brought together; the weight cannot be reduced very much if the recoil is to be kept within bounds so the gain in handling qualities is not very great, although it is true that some single-barrelled guns are superlatively balanced.

22

Fitting a Gun

A man may shoot expertly without knowing anything of the fascinating art of fitting a gun to its owner, but it is an interesting subject complicated by the fact that two different experts may recommend two different stocks to the same shooter. The resulting heartburning and vilification is understandable, but it is really a matter for surprise that it does not happen more often, although some knowledge of the subject is necessary to appreciate that both prescriptions were probably right.

Let us go back to the days before try-guns were available and consider what happened when an untrained man, with no bad habits, was fitted by an old-time expert. This expert would take a good look at him from the gun-maker's standpoint and if he were of ordinary size and build he would prescribe an ordinary stock saying, in effect, 'That is the correct stock for you. Mould your handling of the gun to suit it.' If the customer had some significant difference from the ordinary build, perhaps an unusually long neck, the maker would vary the ordinary stock to allow for it, but the principle that a man without bad habits will shoot well in an orthodox style with an orthodox stock adapted to his physical shape was held to be true. In fact it is true to this day and there are still some experts who rely on this method and produce excellent results.

A try-gun gives the fitter another instrument but it does not provide a magic route to success. Essentially it is an ordinary gun, with joints which allow alterations to be made to the bend and cast-off, and with sliding extensions which permit adjustment of the length of the stock and of the height of the comb. Thus equipped the fitter sets the adjustments in accordance with his estimate of the customer's needs and watches him shoot with it. The shooting may be done at a fixed point, but some believe that the true man is only revealed in the heat of action. I myself find it very difficult to shoot in my normal style at fixed targets, and a fitter learns more of my real needs from seeing me shoot at a variety of clays.

The upshot is that the fitter may alter the stock in accordance with a revised estimate of the shooter's physical needs but never, at this stage, to compensate for faults in the man's style. The reason is that the man should correct faults of style if this is humanly possible, and that is one reason for my urging every beginner to cultivate a good style from the outset. But bad habits are difficult to eradicate, and although an expert fitter would not contemplate altering a stock to compensate for a novice's faults a time will come when he must consider doing so if the customer has done any amount of shooting. This is one of the great partings of the ways where the greatest experts may choose differently, for the stock will be altered only if the fitter believes it to be the lesser evil.

To emphasize how difficult this decision is, and to illustrate how ingrained habits return under stress after their apparent cure, there is the story of a soldier who shot from his left shoulder with a gun in civil life but who taught himself to use a bolt-action rifle as a right-handed man does when he joined the Army. Five years and much shooting after he made the change a crisis called for a very quick shot and, though he was holding his rifle as a right-hander does, he contrived to whip it to his left shoulder and to fire while grasping it in the left-handed manner. The point is not that he hit the target, although he did, but that under stress he discarded an acquired characteristic and reverted to his natural style as a reflex action.

It is not always realized that if a man is standing sideways, with his left shoulder towards the target, he needs a longer stock than he does if his hips and shoulders are at right angles to the target. Since a man shooting game must often adopt one stance for the first barrel and the other for the second the gunmaker can do no more than provide a stock which is a sensible compromise between the two lengths, and the man should be versatile enough to adapt himself to the slight misfit. The weight of the gun also affects the ideal length of the stock; the general rule is that a heavier gun calls for a shorter stock, but this is modified by the balance of the gun. If it is heavy at the muzzle the man will tend to straighten his left arm and then he will require a shorter stock than he would if the gun were heavy at the butt.

Something of the same sort affects both bend and cast-off so it is not really a cause for surprise that two experts, faced by all these variables, should sometimes arrive at different compromises for the same shooter.

One of the difficulties of shooting with a borrowed gun will be minimized if the shooter knows that he can overcome a fault in the length of the stock by pulling his left hand back if the stock is too long, or pushing it forward if the stock is too short; but this has a greater importance. If he is using a stock of sensible length he will slide his left hand up and down unconsciously to compensate for misfits caused by changes of stance, provided that his arm is normally slightly bent. He cannot make such adjustments if his left arm is usually either perfectly straight or extravagantly bent, and that is why the normal grip should be between the two with space for adjustment in either direction.

By the same token both the bend and the cast-off which are ideal when the man is in one position are less than perfect when he is in another, but the defects will be made good by unconscious changes of posture if the man is comfortably balanced and free from muscular constraint. If there are any contortions, muscular tensions or loss of balance these instinctive corrections cannot be made and the standard of shooting will fall.

The foundations of the saying that a good shot can shoot well with any gun are that an experienced man knows what changes in grip and stance will compensate for certain misfits, and if he does in fact make those changes he will shoot well with an ill-fitting gun. But although he may make the changes when he has time to think he is quite exceptional if he does not revert to his natural style as soon as he is hurried, excited or, above all, frightened. As soon as conscious thought gives way to instinctive action the corrections are not made and the shooting reflects the real fit of the gun. The soldier who switched in a flash from right-handed to left was an extreme example of reversion to natural style under stress, but the gunmaker knows that this can happen and is chary of trying to alter ingrained habits.

The wisest course, both in theory and in practice, is to fit the gun to the man when he is in the positions most natural to him provided only that the fundamentals are correct: the barrels must not be canted, the butt must be bedded firmly into the shoulder and so on. This will eliminate all the variations of natural style except those enforced by changes of stance, and even these can be minimized by avoiding exaggerations of any kind. No one style is suitable for tall and short, thickset and slim, but from the very outset each man should cultivate a good style in the middle of the range for his build, and his gun should be fitted to this style.

I value expert fitting so highly that I go to the equivalent of Harley Street for it, but it is very hard to value it in terms of money and performance. Any one man's performance is better with a well fitted 'second' gun than with an ill-fitting 'best', but good fitting is inextricably mixed with good handling qualities. Everyone recognizes good handling qualities, and gunmakers have been building them into guns for generations, for some of the old flintlocks handle beautifully, but unless the terms 'radius of gyration' and 'moment of inertia' really mean something to you it is better not to attempt to understand the theory of fast-handling qualities. Handling is at its fastest when the centre of gravity is between the hands, but closer to the right hand, and when the radius of gyration is at its minimum. Guns which are not of 'best' quality often have enough of the basic necessities of good handling qualities to justify the expense of top-class fitting, but this may not be true of many 'lending' guns.

A well-fitted gun with even average handling qualities opens up an entirely new vista to many people; it has little noticeable weight, and just points where you are looking without conscious effort on your part.

23

The Kick of Guns

The kick of a 12-bore should be treated with respect but without fear. If the grip, stance and mounting are reasonably correct the kick will not be noticed, but the man who trifles with it will soon have a headache and memorable bruises on his shoulder, jaw and fingers. Gun shops do have gadgets by the dozen to minimize the bruises, but the proper cure is to hold and mount the gun correctly. A rubber band held between the teeth is the traditional preventive for a gun-headache but setting the muscles of the neck and jaw is far better. Rubber rings on trigger guards, rubber tubing on triggers and top levers bent sideways are all palliatives. They mitigate the symptoms without curing the disease. Rubber pads fixed permanently to the butt escape this censure because their purpose is to mould themselves to the shape of the shoulder and to prevent the butt slipping when the first barrel is fired, rather than to absorb recoil.

If we held and mounted our guns perfectly we should be able to fire many hundreds of cartridges in a day without ill effects, but no-one does and the discomforts are the measure of our failings.

Nevertheless I greatly prefer to give lightly-loaded cartridges to an absolute beginner and am convinced that every woman and young boy should get used to a ·410 before firing anything bigger. The point is that flinching from the recoil is a habit which is very easy to acquire but very, very difficult to get rid of. It is much better to allow a raw beginner to concentrate on the essentials without a nagging fear at the back of his mind that he may get hurt.

A mild case of flinching can often be cured by loading a fired cartridge surreptitiously and letting the pupil laugh himself out of it, but for anything more serious it is wise to use a ·410. This tiny cartridge cannot hurt anybody, but it breaks clays and the pupil gets the idea that if he can do this with a miniature gun he might become something rather good with a full-sized one. Ambition overpowers the fear of pain and flinching disappears if, but only if, the remedy is applied before the habit is ingrained.

The smaller guns, 16- and 20-bores, do not necessarily kick less than 12-bores. For any given weight of shot, sent off at a given velocity, the kick of the gun is related to its weight and some of the very light small-bores kick like mules. However, there is no need to labour the point, because in general a man will not be hurt by a 12-bore of normal weight if the load of shot is no greater than seven-eighths of an ounce, while neither a woman nor a boy will come to much harm firing a 20-bore with eleven-sixteenths of an ounce of shot if they are used to handling a ·410.

In the very early stages beginners often flinch from the noise of the gun but this disappears very quickly, particularly if there is the fun of seeing the shot hit something. For this reason it is helpful to arrange for the very first shots to be fired from a bridge at sticks floating in water. Then the novice gets the feel of the triggers and of the recoil while learning the size of the pattern, but the unpleasant effects of the noise and the kick are ignored in the excitement of seeing where the shot goes.

This whole business of using light loads only applies to novices in the very early stages; once they have cut their teeth, as it were, it is much better to use normal loads and to let the gun teach the novice that it must be respected. Most people get over-confident at some stage and then learn from the bruises.

24

Proof Marks

Proof marks are important to everyone who owns, fires, buys, sells, lends or even stands near a gun. Hallmarks on the family silver may be taken for granted, but to ignore proof marks is always dangerous and is often illegal. They are one of the things of which everyone should have a working knowledge and it is quite enough for a layman to have an up-to-date reference book if he uses it with the knowledge first that modern cartridges demand modern proof marks, and second that a gun can get out of proof.

What is not enough is a hasty glance at some half-comprehended marks and a bland assumption that all is well and will be so for ever. That this is not realized by people who should know better was brought home to me most forcibly when I picked up the remains of a best gun which had been broken in a traffic accident, and saw that it had been proofed for black powder only, even though it had been used with nitro cartridges for at least two generations. Of course the gun might have come through re-proofing in the nitro era with flying colours, but that would have been a long time ago, since the barrels were worn to the thickness of paper. The gun had been made by a very famous maker in 1888 and had passed from one keen shooting generation of the same family to another ever since. I had seen it myself in most effective action for 20 years. That it had withstood forces for which it was never designed or intended speaks volumes for the maker but, in one respect, it is a pity that it did not burst.

Because that gun was so incredibly staunch sceptics can say 'Well it did not burst in the field, even though it had manifestly been out

98

of proof for years, so the Proof Houses must demand an unnecessarily high factor of safety', and it is true that the laws governing proof defeat their own purpose to some extent by demanding such a high standard that people do not send their guns for re-proofing as often as they should. Very often a gun is a member of the household, as a dog or a horse may be, and the line of thought runs something like this: 'That gun is a thoroughbred and in perfect condition; the barrels shine like the moon and the action is as tight as can be. It has been doing its job perfectly since my grandfather's time and it is ludicrous to insist that it should be tested now. No fuddy-duddy gun-smith or Proof House shall set rapacious hands upon it for they will blind me with science to make a job for themselves.' I do not con-done such thinking, it is utterly wrong, but it is understandable, even if it is no less dangerous than the man who will not allow his gun to be re-proofed because he knows that it will fail. Such a man ties his gun to a gate, fires some heavily-loaded cartridges by remote control and, if it still works, blithely uses it for the rest of his life. He usually gets away with it, the gun does not burst, the belief that the Proof Houses are over-strict gains ground and the law falls further into disrepute.

Nevertheless, it is an essential and excellent law which should be respected, studied and observed. Perhaps, like most things, it is less than perfect; certainly it could have a warmer image with advantage, but it is the best available to us and it is all that stands between shooting men and charlatans of a most dangerous kind. Re-proofing is remarkably cheap and ensures that the gun is safe for use with the prescribed loads; surely it is idiotic to endanger one's left hand, or life itself, to save a few pence and a little trouble.

Modern British marks include the maximum length of the cartridge and the allowable working pressure within the barrel. It is as stupid to use more powerful cartridges as it is to overload a bridge, although such cartridges will usually enter the chamber. Everyone should know that although British cartridges are regulated to conform to British proof certain foreign brands generate higher pressures and overstress our guns. Unfortunately the older British marks do not give the same details and they are confusing because they have a family likeness although they are different. There are, for instance, at least five different British marks for nitro proof but it is the absence of any of them which indicates that the gun was tested for black powder only. Further, foreign countries have their own standards and marks which are different from ours, so the layman's only recourse is a reference book. Should he not be satisfied that his gun has marks covering the cartridges he intends to use he should ask a gunsmith.

The marks only indicate the gun's condition at the time of testing and every gun will get out of proof if given enough use, while a few weeks of neglect will reduce the best to rubbish. Corrosion starts the instant the gases touch the metal, rust is an ever-present menace, a tiny fraction of metal is removed by every shot that is fired and even legitimate cleaning rubs away a little more. We just have to face the fact that guns have a limited life and ensure that we discard them before they destroy us. Given proper care their life is very long; tales are told of guns which have fired more than a million rounds, but a vandal who uses emery paper to remove the fruits of neglect will destroy his gun in no time. Even metal polish should not be used to restore the brightness of a tarnished surface, for one has only to think of an old soldier's buttons to realize that its repeated use rubs away a lot of metal. The wear can be gauged by measurement alone, time is not the dominant factor, and when the wear has reached the prescribed limit the gun should be re-proofed. The action may be tight and smooth, and the barrels will shine like a looking-glass if they have been well cared for, but the steel of the barrels may be perilously thin.

Much interesting and authoritative information about proof marks and kindred matters is contained in *Notes on the Proof of Shot Guns and other Small Arms* which can be obtained from the Proof House, 48 Commercial Road, London E.1. I do not suggest that the advice given to a layman by any reputable member of the gun trade would be misleading or insufficient but it is not until one studies a work of this kind that one appreciates the multitude of the pitfalls.

25

The Care of a Gun

Although it is true that sufficient firing will wear out any gun the vast majority come to their ends through inadequate cleaning or rough handling long before they are shot out. Let us deal with cleaning first and consider what should be done as a matter of routine every time a gun has been out of the house, whether it has been fired or not.

First wipe the outside with a dry rag and take the gun to pieces, then roll a piece of newspaper into a loose ball as big as the top joint of your thumb and push it through each barrel to get rid of the worst of the dirt. This is only to keep the main cleaning kit nice, and we are now ready to start serious work by putting a jag on to the cleaning rod, wrapping a piece of flannel round it and pushing it through each barrel about five times. Then substitute a bronze brush with a little oil on it for the jag and give the barrels a good scrub; push a dry rag through again to wipe off the oil and loose dirt and look carefully through the barrels *from both ends.* If they are not as bright as the moon go on with the bronze brush and dry rag until they really shine and then clean the valleys on either side of both ribs with a rag folded over a matchstick. The main object is to ensure that no water stays there. Push back the extractors and clean the surfaces thus exposed and then the whole of the outside of the barrels; these can then be put aside for the moment.

Use an old tooth brush to clean the chequer work on the fore-end and a dry rag on the metal parts, taking pains to get into all the nooks and corners. Then do the same with the stock, taking particular care to clean all the dried oil from the inaccessible places. The gun will now be clean and it only remains to oil it.

I use Young's ·303 oil inside the barrels and Three-in-One on all the other metal. The plan is to make an unbroken film of oil between the metal and the air, but it is important that too much oil should not get into the locks, so do not be over-generous. A common mistake is to put so much oil on the woodwork that it swells and causes all kinds of trouble. A trace of oil on the woodwork will keep it bright. but wax furniture polish is really better.

That is ordinary, routine cleaning, and if you have three cleaning rods and the rag cut to size you can do the job perfectly in about three minutes, but if a gun has been out in heavy rain or, worse, has salt, mud and sea-water on it, you must wash off every trace of salt, dry everything and then do a routine cleaning. There is one, and only one, correct way to dry the barrels. This is to pour five pints of boiling water through them, shake the surplus water off and hang them up on a loop of string tied round the lumps. The heat in the metal will soon evaporate all the moisture. Shake the fore-end before drying all the nooks with a rag and then deal with the stock, which is much the hardest part. Grasp the small of the stock with both hands and shake it vigorously; an astonishingly large amount of water may come out. Then dry it with rags and a short blast from a hair dryer or the exhaust end of a vacuum cleaner; feathers are helpful at this stage for the crevices. When the gun is as dry as possible clean it in the routine way and leave it in pieces in a warm, not hot, place overnight. Another routine cleaning in the morning will ensure that nothing was overlooked.

Some people take out the extractors and the bottom plate of a box-lock, or the locks of a sidelock, but in my opinion you may do more harm than good *in this country* unless you have the proper screw-drivers and some skill, especially if you send your gun to the maker at the end of every season anyway. If you shoot in the wet tropics it is essential to undo the screws and to be careful about the perspiration on your hands, for perspiration is highly corrosive.

If the barrels have been heated by a lot of shooting, perhaps at clays, it is a good plan to wipe them out before they cool and to oil them very heavily. I have a theory that gun oil neutralizes corrosive substances which enter the pores of heated metal and sweat out over the following two or three days, but this is only my own theory.

The cleaning described above will keep guns in good condition for generations in this country and the only remaining question is 'How much more can an amateur legitimately do if things go wrong?' Turpentine helps to remove lead; a steel wire brush on the inside of the barrels can be used and, once in a lifetime, we might stretch a point and use metal polish in the same place. But that is about all; if repeated routine cleaning will not remove a blemish it is better to leave it to a professional.

Some people may wonder if all this cleaning is worth the trouble. Would it not be better to do less cleaning and to replace the gun more often? They may be right, but I buy the best gun I can afford and treasure it; then I have a thoroughbred all my life instead of a series of things in which I can take no pride.

Experts tell us that guns keep better in a rack than in a case, but if they must live in cases it is essential that the baize is perfectly dry.

Although I treasure my gun at home I hold firmly to the belief that a treasured weapon is no weapon at all. In the field it must stand up to the stresses of weather and fair usage, and I should replace any gun which could not. In point of fact guns resemble many highly specialized things in that they are very strong to resist the stresses they were made to withstand, but very weak in other respects. Barrels contain great pressures from within but are easily dented by a blow from the outside; no amount of fair handling ever broke the small of a stock but many have been snapped when the butt has been used to finish off a wounded rabbit.

Above all no gun can resist a bending force, which can be applied all too easily in a car. In fact cars are so productive of accidents to guns that I prefer to have mine in its case when it is inside the car and in my own hands when it is outside. One often sees an assembled gun placed on the roof of a stationary car to be out of the way, but every season some unthinking person drives off and his gun falls to the ground. Those left leaning against a fence can be knocked over by dogs and the number damaged while getting in and out of Land-Rovers must be enormous. Any obstruction in the barrel, even a little water, will cause a bulge if the gun is fired and neither a bulge nor a dent should be neglected. Repeated firing will enlarge the bulge or rub metal from the underside of a dent and makes repairs more difficult, so a damaged barrel should not be fired.

Some readers will recall that soldiers were trained to toss their rifles over a hedge to a comrade who caught them on the far side. It is a very quick way of getting armed men over a hedge but I have never had enough confidence in the other man's catching ability to toss my own gun over.

No matter how careful one is there is always a danger from mud; one should not fall over, stumble or contrive to jab the muzzle into a bank, but most of us have done all these things at least once and the very first action which should be taken after regaining one's feet is to look through the barrels to make sure that they are clear. Every experienced man sees that the barrels are not obstructed by mud, water or anything else before he loads a gun after any pause in the firing as well as at the beginning of shooting. Provided that the obstruction is seen there is no cause for alarm; a hazel stick will serve as a ramrod and a pull-through can be improvised from a piece of string and a handkerchief, but to spring to one's feet after a stumble and go straight into action is folly. Apart from worn barrels the commonest cause of bursts is almost certainly mud scooped into the muzzle during some trifling mishap and the lesson to be learned is self-evident.

Most people know that a 20-bore cartridge will slide down the chamber of a 12-bore until the rim catches on the cone. There it lurks, just in front of the chamber, waiting for a 12-bore cartridge to be fired behind it and the prospect of the two going off together is so frightening that some people will not allow 20-bore cartridges to enter the house. I have no first-hand knowledge of the damage caused by firing one cartridge on top of another, but the fact that most of us know of the possibility ensures that care is taken.

26

Bad Cartridges and Good

I have never had a misfire in a shotgun myself and I do not know of any recommended drill to cope with the eventuality, but having been present when the problem has arisen I am quite certain that the most important thing is to keep one's head. After all, the problem arose many times with all the small arms we encountered in the Army and all we ever did was to eject the dud round and carry on. The following seems a sensible routine for dealing with a misfire; unless the cartridge has a stout metal case the time of danger will be so short that it can be ignored.

Danger only arises if the cap has been struck but the charge has failed to explode, for it may be 'hanging fire'. That is to say it may be smouldering inside and liable to explode at any moment, but it does not matter if it goes off in the chamber with the breech closed because, trained to be safe with guns, we keep the muzzle pointed safely at all times. Neither does it matter if it goes off outside the chamber and well away from breakables. Then it has no more power than a small firework and is probably harmless if it is fifteen yards away. There is danger only during the brief time it takes to open the gun and throw the cartridge fifteen yards, but of course you must not be in line with the barrels while the breech is open in case the dud chooses that moment to go off and comes flying out backwards.

As it could not take more than two seconds to snap the gun open and throw the cartridge fifteen yards one should wait a sensible time before doing just that, and the only question is 'How long is sensible?' The answer is that if you think that 10 to 1 gives you a good enough chance wait twenty seconds before you open the gun, but if fifty to 1 is more to your taste wait a hundred seconds. Having cleared the gun you must not fail to look through the barrels because a weak cartridge may have left the wads inside.

Being a good citizen I should make a point some time later of finding the cartridge I threw away and disposing of it safely either by burying it or by throwing it into permanent water, but I should have a good look at the indentation on the cap first to see if the striker was at fault. If the same barrel misfired twice with decent cartridges I should seek a gunmaker's advice and be prepared to bet that the gun was defective.

Never buy cheap cartridges which do not come from manufacturers of high repute; it is short-sighted to do so. All cartridges contain an explosive and the means of igniting it in a fairly foolproof package, but there is an inescapable element of danger and it is not a reassuring thought that materials or workmanship may have been scamped to save a few pence on a box. With good cartridges it is usually true that a miss is the shooter's own fault and, anyway, the cost of cartridges is almost the smallest part of the cost of shooting game. There is no need to pay fancy prices, for the extra cost reflects the case rather than the contents, but buy from sources of such long-standing repute that all dangers of faulty manufacture can be ignored.

There are many anecdotes to the effect that good shots use the standard, cheap cartridges while those who have doubts about their skill use the more expensive brands and in general I would agree that this is so, but there are legitimate exceptions: paper cases swell if they get damp and it is wise to have some water-resistant cases for use in wet weather even though they are more costly. If I want to shoot at the peak of my form I use an ounce and an eighth of shot instead of the usual ounce and a sixteenth; the extra 6% may not make an atom of difference but it gives me confidence. Also, cartridges loaded with slightly less than an ounce of shot are perfectly effective against most driven game and they are much less tiring if more than, say, 150 are to be fired in a few hours. I do not mind getting tired in a good cause, but fatigue causes shooting performance to drop sharply and to that I take the gravest exception, so for a hectic day against driven game I use lightly-loaded cartridges. I generally use them up on pigeon at the end of the season and find that they kill the same as the heaviest loads—well, nearly the same.

As long as a shotgun is used for its primary purpose, which is as

a short-ranged weapon of opportunity, I really believe that the confidence of the man is much more important than the precise contents of the cartridge he fires. If he thinks that such and such a load
is best then, for him, it is the best.

It is when people try to get the limit of performance from a gun
that trouble starts and wide differences of opinion arise. We are all
agreed that a 3-inch magnum with big shot will reach higher into
the sky for geese than most cartridges, but informed men do not
agree how big the shot should be, and I know knowledgeable men
who use anything from BB to number 3 shot. But is even that flexible
enough? In good light I shoot for the head and neck of a goose and,
having killed them with every size of shot from number 7 to BB,
I respect the opinions of the well-informed but I keep an open mind.
In the dark, when I have been compelled to go for the body, I have
never killed a goose with shot smaller than number 4.

In general it is folly to use cartridges longer than those which your
gun was chambered to take, even though they will drop in nicely.
In the ordinary way there is insufficient space for the crimp to get
out of the way of the wad so the pressure rises until the wad is forced
through or the gun either swells or bursts. Even if the built-in factor
of safety enables the gun to take the extra stress without permanent
damage you have taken a risk without a chance of profit because the
pattern will probably be spoiled. There are exceptions to this and
it is possible, in the interests of standardization, to use one case and
slow-burning powders for different lengths of chamber without taking
risks.

If the shooting of the day is to be concentrated on hares I use
number 4 shot to minimize wounding and for snipe I use number 8;
for all other inland shooting except geese I use number 6 shot. I claim
no magic for 6s, and the probability is that 5s or 7s would do just as
well. It is true that larger shot will kill at slightly longer ranges but
I do not automatically use them either for rough shooting or on the
foreshore. By far the best remedy for wild birds is the increased
stealth and knowledge that will enable the man to shoot at normal
ranges. Only when all possibilities of cunning have been exhausted
do I use larger shot and then nothing bigger than number 4. Like
everyone else I have experimented with high-velocity cartridges; if
you think that you do better with them stick to them by all means
but the normal load at normal velocity suits most people best.

27

Clothes and Accessories

If we did all our shooting in warm, dry weather and only walked over short, smooth grass we should be perfectly clad for performance, comfort and smartness in a tweed shooting suit, shoes, stockings and either a hat or a cap. When our predecessors evolved this most practical dress (and it only became fashionable because it is so eminently serviceable) a proper suit was worn, but now a coat of one tweed is often used with breeches of another because this conceals the shooter better.

Shoes are preferable to boots because foot-work is of first importance and a man shooting well in clumsy gum-boots would do so much better in something lighter. In practice boots of some kind are usually essential, the lightest which will stand up to the ground over which you expect to walk. Any leather boots of reasonable quality can be made waterproof and beautifully supple by soaking them, almost to saturation point, in castor oil or liquid dubbin. My present pair soaked up nine ounces of oil before I put them on and they have not let in one drop of water during the two seasons I have used them. Newmarket boots have merit if you must walk through brambles and some people speak well of the boots which resemble them but have thin rubber uppers instead of canvas.

Brambles and wet kale mark the watershed where the choice has to be made between utility and smartness. Puttees, anklets and gaiters of leather or canvas each have their own merits, and in really thick undergrowth I have been glad of the protection given by beaters' leggings.

A hat is better than a cap in the rain but it is scraped off more often by undergrowth. Something should always be worn on the head because all game, except possibly pheasants, tends to swerve away from a bare-headed man and he will get materially less shooting than he would if his head were covered.

The first big problem arises when rain comes: if you put a raincoat over your ordinary clothes your gun will fit less well. If it is humanly possible I take a raincoat off before firing begins but I have a golfer's windcheater which I can wear over my coat without affecting the fit of the gun. Special jackets are made for shooting from Grenfell cloth or something similar, and as they are both waterproof and warm one can dispense with a tweed coat and wear them whatever the weather. They are very serviceable but some hosts do not look upon them with kindness on more formal occasions.

You may look very smart if your clothes are well tailored but you cannot shoot your best if your coat is the least bit tight. You must have complete freedom from the waist up and a coat will be about right if it fits nicely when you are wearing two thick, long-sleeved jerseys. Then you only wear one of the jerseys for shooting and have the freedom you need without distressing the tailor. Ideally both the coat and the windcheater should have raglan shoulders and very wide armholes, elbows and cuffs. Tailors seem to have something against raglan shoulders and to prefer pleats of their own devising but, for shooting, all substitutes for raglan shoulders are inferior.

Concealment and warmth often demand special clothes for shooting wildfowl and pigeon, and in very cold weather these may interfere with good shooting, but I think that I know how to cope with the coldest conditions elsewhere without reducing effectiveness. The basic idea is to wear as much as you like below the waist but to maintain freedom of movement and the fit of the gun above it. My own maximum above the waist is a silk vest, a woollen vest, a woollen shirt, one jersey, a tweed coat and a golfer's windcheater. The fit of the windcheater is vital: it is big enough to allow free movement but fits closely enough to let me mount my gun without rumpling up and catching the butt; being made of Grenfell cloth it is both wind and waterproof. Below the waist put on as many layers as you like, but let the first be a pair of natural silk, women's stockings (they are surprisingly warm) and let the last be a pair of golfer's overtrousers which are both wind and waterproof.

It is a good idea to wear golf mittens while shooting and to slip on a pair of big leather mitts between drives. In complete privacy one can profit greatly from a woollen helmet. Most of these bits and pieces can be packed into a spare cartridge bag if the weather changes.

I say a spare cartridge bag because I will have nothing to do with cartridge belts or tubes. If you have no loader the right-hand pocket of your coat, which should be lined with chamois leather, is the best place for cartridges, and if you put the bag somewhere safe on reaching your stand and replenish your pocket as necessary, you will reload far faster than a man who has his cartridges in a tube or belt. The best bags are made from pigskin; mine holds a hundred cartridges and has a hard rim so that the mouth is always open.

Everyone should have a cartridge extractor, to pull out a swollen case, a pocket knife and a piece of string, but those are the only gadgets which you need habitually carry. In cold weather a hand guard to slide over the barrels to protect your left hand from their chill is useful. A shooting stick is a great asset if you can sit on it but is an unmitigated nuisance if you have to carry it when you are a walking gun.

Some men carry enough gadgets to cover a Christmas tree but let us examine their real usefulness. Of whistles, pegs, leads and all things pertaining to restraining wild dogs, it is true that it is better to peg an unsteady dog down than to tether it to your waist, but it is much, much better to leave it at home unless you bring a handler. Game can hear a whistle just as well as the dog can and it would work to hand signals if perfect.

'Priests,' and all the devices for dispatching wounded game, are unnecessary if you know how to do it properly. If you have only one hand free tuck your thumb under a bird's beak and curl your fore-finger round the back of its skull; then turn your wrist so that the bird's breast is away from you and give a flick, down and up again, as if you were cracking a tiny whip. Too strong a flick will break its head right off and it needs a little practice. With both hands available you can enclose the wings and hit the back of the bird's head against anything hard, your boot or a tree perhaps, by swinging your arms. You can crush the top of the skull of most young birds by pressing down hard with your thumb. Rabbits and hares are best finished off by grasping the small of the back, not the hind legs, in the left hand and hitting the back of the neck with the edge of your right hand.

CLOTHES AND ACCESSORIES III

If a gun is properly held, mounted and fitted there will be little perceptible recoil and no bruises so there should be no use for all the rubber rings, pads and patches which are on the market.

A 'poacher's pocket' should only be used as a last resort as it is the quickest way of ruining both game and clothes.

Opinions differ sharply as to the size of the flask you should have available and the extent to which it should be used. Try to do as Rome does, but the good shots keep their reflexes sharp until the shooting is over.

All your clothes and kit should be tried and proved before being used for serious work. Boots which cause blisters, straps which break and zip fasteners which come adrift are signs of incompetence. It is just permissible to borrow cartridges if you can repay the loan as soon as you return to your car but you should not need to borrow anything else. This may seem harsh, but the underlying idea is that you are supposed to be able to solve all your own problems without attracting attention. The way this unwritten rule grew up will be clear once you have seen the chaos caused by men who lose one gum-boot in a swamp, have guns which break down, or bring only BB shot for use against driven partridges.

There are two small points which can become important: if you wear braces ensure that the buckle is nowhere near the part of your shoulder touched by the butt, because the cuts and bruises can be severe enough to stop you shooting, and never have anything in the inside pocket of your coat on the right hand side.

Finally, although there is a school of thought which leans towards unorthodox clothes for shooting, have a reflective look at them at the end of a long, hard, wet day. You may agree with me that orthodox clothes stand the strain rather better.

28

Finding Somewhere to Shoot

This may prove to be the most intractable problem of all because several difficulties are intertwined and react upon each other. First and foremost you will be welcome nowhere until you are known to be safe with a gun but you cannot gain this reputation without shooting in public. I was trained and introduced to the shooting world by my father and things will be very much easier if someone will do the same for you.

At the same time one faces the fact that although shooting game should not be competitive a novice has to reach a certain standard before he is acceptable, and it is difficult to get enough practice except at clays. Myxomatosis, which almost wiped out the rabbits twenty years ago, did the novice shooter a great disservice because, for the time being at any rate, their numbers are so reduced that almost the only casual shooting which remains is at pigeon and wild-fowl. In the old days most of us began by shooting rabbits and farmers were glad to be rid of the pestiferous things provided that the novice behaved sensibly. Unhappily the false glamour which sur-rounds poaching has induced so many people to leave the path of rectitude that many landowners regard every man, woman, child and dog as a potential poacher of the blackest shade until they have proved their innocence.

The question of expense runs parallel to all these obstacles and it can be taken as certain that one will put in at least as much as one takes out, but it may be possible to put work rather than cash into a shoot and let us follow up this alternative. If work is exchanged for shooting neither income tax nor insurance stamps erode the results;

the cost of the stamps on the card of every full-time male employee of the shoot is enough to buy all the food required by five hundred pheasants so, when income tax is considered as well, an amateur starts with a big advantage. In other words, a shooter may work his passage with profit to both sides.

In the district in which I live all the Saturdays in February and the first in March are devoted to organized pigeon shooting, and at those times a tactful approach to any landowner, farmer or manager of shooting is least likely to be refused. If the shooter makes a good impression he may be invited to defend the crops against pigeon during the summer, but he should understand clearly that many men are itching to take his place and that he will be welcome only as long as it is apparent to those in authority that the pigeon he kills are more of a nuisance than he is. A dog will bring trouble if it so much as attracts the attention of cows which are in calf or disturbs ewes. A man who brings a gamekeeper, suspecting poachers, hot-foot from the far end of his beat to discover the source of the shooting is inviting banishment and, in general, it is best to give the impression that one is an amiable eccentric who guards the crops with success but spends most of the time doing good turns like rounding up stray bullocks.

Some of the organizations for destroying vermin are short of what they call 'lone shooters' and those who join their ranks can have a worthwhile amount of sport.

If you have no acquaintances in the shooting world you may be able to get some help from the Wildfowlers Association of Great Britain and Ireland (Grosvenor House, 104 Watergate Street, Chester), the British Field Sports Society (26 Caxton Street, London SW2) or the Clay Pigeon Shooting Association (Angel Road, London N18). All these bodies supply information to their members and they are more likely to put you in touch with people who know the ropes than anything else. The local gun club, shooting school or gunsmith may be able to perform the same service.

Before you start thinking in terms of staying in a hotel which advertises shooting as an attraction or taking a gun in, say, a grouse syndicate for a shooting holiday you should give serious consideration to where you want to shoot. I greatly prefer to have sport close to my doorstep, with shooting as a part of my ordinary way of life, rather than that it should be a special occasion. You may have wonderful shooting on a moor six hundred miles from your home but you may spend the bulk of your holiday re-reading the Waverley Novels in an austere lodge while the weather makes shooting impossible. Even if you are invited to join a smart syndicate with congenial members and big bags which shoots one hundred miles from your home you should not accept before thinking about the small concern in your own village. It may seem paradoxical, but much of the enjoyment of shooting comes when you have no gun with you— perhaps from seeing the mallard rearing a brood on a pond or hearing the partridges when you are out for a walk, and it is probably a mistake to sever a local connection.

If the term 'rough shooting' is used in its old fashioned sense, that is to say to mean shooting which derives little or no benefit from a gamekeeper, it describes both the ultimate ambition of many men and an excellent starting point for novices. Apart from any shooting rent the cost may be limited to that of cartridges and the game may be truly wild, but there would be very little to shoot in my part of the world, except pigeon, unless human beings gave some help. However it is so cheap and so easy to increase the stock of game that the general failure to do so can only be attributed to a lack of knowledge of how to set about the task. Please banish all thought of heavy work, expensive equipment and the payment of wages from your mind and substitute the idea that you are going to do no more than swing Nature's balance as far as, say, £5 will move it. Even £1 will make a difference if its weight is put in the right place but a fortune can be spent to no good purpose if the effort is misapplied.

The order of priority should be (a) exclude human trespassers, (b) attack the predators, (c) provide an environment congenial to game and (d) let visiting game find food. Nature's balance is so delicately poised that even if the first two are limited to no more than notices prohibiting entry, shooting all predators on sight and killing some rats with Warfarin, the stock of game will rise, and to understand why this is so the principle of the shootable surplus must be grasped. Imagine that fifty pheasants are confined in a pen but that they are only given enough food for thirty every day: it is evident that no more than thirty can survive to breed next year and that this number will be no less if some are shot before they starve. Every piece of land has a certain amount of natural food which is available for game and, subject to disturbance and destruction by predators, the stock of game which can be supported by that natural food will move in. If the conditions suit them the birds will take up residence. If the supply of natural food is increased by even one sack of corn the amount of game will rise by an equivalent amount.

The common mistake is to get the priorities wrong. If rats and foxes find that free meals are to be had on your ground, and if crows and magpies eat the eggs and chicks of the game, the corn will have gone for nothing. Neither will you profit if the game is constantly disturbed by picnic parties, but given shelter, peace and quiet and freedom from predators game will fill any land to the limit of the food available. Pigeon, mallard and pheasants respond to the smallest help and both novices and old hands may well be best rewarded by renting a piece of land and working on the lines described.

The greatest reward in shooting for money spent of which I have known was obtained by feeding an ornamental lake to induce duck to nest and then augmenting their numbers by attracting migrants with additional food. The most certain route to failure is to antagonize your neighbours by giving the impression that you are trying to lure away their game by lavish feeding.

It is very difficult to obtain accurate costs from sufficient shoots to be certain of the facts but the following should be fairly representative of the 1972 prices of formal shooting if it is assumed that the full market price is paid for rent, wages, food and all ancillary items. A shoot which concentrates on driven pheasants will spend between £4 and £7 for each pheasant which goes into the bag. This treats all ground game, duck, pigeon and woodcock as a cost-free bonus: the wide range of costs seems to be due in part to the different rents paid and in part to the varying proportions of hand-reared birds. The cost of partridges may be about 40% to 60% of that of pheasants in the same area, while the rent of a grouse moor may be something like £6 or £7 for each brace expected.

No charge for rent normally appears in the accounts of a man who shoots over his own land, and most shoots grow at least a proportion of the corn fed to the game, but anyone thinking of taking a gun in a syndicate, or of running his own shooting on a considerable scale, should have the overall costs in mind. If the cost of rent is excluded wages absorb between 50% and 60% of the funds of a pheasant shoot which rears on an average scale, when the work is done by professionals.

There is not much useful advice to be given about wildfowling on the foreshore. Locating available shooting is largely a matter of using the opportunities presented by local knowledge, personal contacts, membership of clubs or advertisements. Having found the place the best thing is to obtain a guide with extensive local knowledge and to make a study of tide-tables and the combinations of weather, moon, tide and local conditions which give you the best chance. People tend to be very secretive, and this is understandable where accessible areas are heavily over-shot, but perseverance will yield something.

Part Three

In The Shooting Field

29

Walking-up for Beginners

Shooting driven game is something of a gala occasion for ordinary mortals and very few of us live at that level all the time. We remember the days of driving; when we meet our shooting friends we talk about them because they are the notable events. But the ordinary fare, the shooting which provides the fun day in and day out, is walking-up, wildfowling and shooting pigeon. It is on these lesser days, when we have time to stop, stare and notice, that the ways of game can be learned and a man's speed of reaction can be sharpened.

It is perfectly true that a great deal can be learned at a modern shooting school, and I count myself among their staunchest advocates, but they cannot fill the gap in a man's shooting education exemplified by the following. A snipe rises in front of a novice, he is taken by surprise and does not recognize it for a moment, then, moving clumsily because he has the wrong foot in front, he fires. Contrast this with the reaction of an old hand who knows that a snipe is rising as soon as he hears the 'scaarp' and starts to mount his gun at once. By the time he sees the bird the gun is in more or less the right direction and half-way to his shoulder; then, jink as it may, that snipe is in mortal danger. It is not so much that the old hand moved faster but that he started earlier and did everything correctly at the first attempt. Moreover, experience had taught him that a snipe was to be expected in a place like that, so he had a double advantage.

This matter of being ready, recognizing the quarry and starting early runs right through game shooting, and one hallmark of a good shot is that he always seems to have plenty of time. He is probably not blessed with the split-second reflexes of a fly-weight boxer, and his gun may be less than a perfect fit, but he is yards faster than anyone who has not been schooled by hours of walking-up and waiting for game.

The first rule of walking-up is DON'T TALK, and calling dogs counts as talking. The human voice is dreaded by most wild things and it carries for surprising distances. It is also vital to realize that wildlife is wary and good at self-preservation, so a certain degree of stealth and cunning is essential. If you walk alone along a hedge the probability is that any game there will either run away along the hedge, hide or fly out on the other side, so you will not get a shot, but if you put a 'stop' at the end of the hedge (a piece of paper or a coat will serve), game will not run past it; a dog working the hedge will flush anything which tries to hide, and a friend on the far side will have a chance at anything hidden from you.

You may be able to flush partridges within range from stubble or grass but they will often rise too far away or run through the hedge. The best tactics are to start at the boundary and to work them into roots, potatoes or anywhere there is cover, but before you walk the cover, take thought. All game prefers to fly downwind and downhill but they are wise enough to run away along the rows if you let them and they are very good at hiding. It always pays to move slowly rather than fast, and although in the open you can cover the ground widely-spaced and at a relatively brisk pace, in any cover you should be close together and move slowly. A covey will probably rise as one party from the open, but when separated in cover they tend to leave in ones and twos—if you say nothing, not one single word.

Picking up the game which has been shot is easy in the open, but you should know how to mark birds which fall in cover. Let us consider the hardest case, which is when you are alone and have no dog. You drop a partridge close to a big yellow leaf, but as you go forward a rabbit makes you take your eye off the spot and then you see dozens of big yellow leaves and you never find the partridge. What you should have done was to get a *bearing* and a *distance* from the spot on which you were standing when you fired, and to have marked that spot. Suppose you leave your hat where you fired and suppose that the bird fell forty yards out in line with a pylon; you go along the line searching and counting your steps. If when you have covered 40 yards you have not found the partridge you mark the place with a handkerchief. A good search all round the handkerchief yields nothing but you are not beaten; just go back to your hat, check the bearing and try again keeping in mind that we tend to over-estimate distances and that your forty yards may have been no more than twenty-five or thirty.

If you had a companion he should have got a cross-bearing onto your bird and he should have stood still as you went forward. Then he can direct you as an umpire at cricket gives a batsman his guard; you stay on your bearing while he directs you onto his. The bird should be where they cross, but it may have struggled under cover and still require a bit of a search. There are variations of this method involving lines through two prominent objects, but the same idea lies behind them all.

If you have a dog do remember that you smell much more than any game bird even if you have just had six baths, so keep downwind and give him plenty of room. Do not distract him and let him use his nose; trust his nose, for it may well be that he knows more of the problem in hand than you do. If he fails your chances are not spoiled by his efforts, but you can ruin his.

All this time you are absorbing useful knowledge without realizing it. Now you keep your balance while walking through turnips; you distinguish between a wood-pigeon and a rock dove without conscious thought, you mount your gun automatically when a magpie, jay or stoat appears but you do not react to fieldfares and the like. You never mistake a leveret for a rabbit now, and the burble of a mallard drake brings you to action stations. All this may sound elementary, and to some extent it is, but it is training which every shooting man should have. The half-seen flicker of brown, to which an experienced man reacts because he knows that only a woodcock looks like that, means nothing to a novice, so the one gets a shot while the other never so much as knows that shootable game was about.

Sometimes things which are not supposed to be shot suffer for looking too much like game. Little owls can look very like 'cock from a certain angle, and most youngsters have shot a September owl. The latter is a young pheasant shot before the first of October in the belief that it was a partridge—it should never happen, but it does.

This strolling with a gun has a charm of its own, and if you have a gun in your hands for an hour or so on most days of the week you will shoot far, far better than if you only see your gun on major occasions. Most of us find out the elements of the ways of game and predators when idling with a gun and it is a remarkably pleasant way of learning.

30

More Advanced Walking-up

While one is learning to react quickly to half-seen glimpses of shoot-able game one should be developing a sixth sense which signals where game is likely to be and what it will do. Of course it is not really an extra sense but a fund of knowledge upon which one draws with-out thinking. It is in the bones of every man who was brought up among game, but it can be learned by anyone who asks himself why such and such did that in those conditions. An out-and-out novice would make little progress without any guidance, but once he has grasped the fundamentals of food, shelter, weather and season he probably learns more quickly alone, provided that he appreciates that the influence of each factor varies. Thus, early in September an isolated oak tree may be chiefly important for the fact that it is likely to turn partridges this way or that with the wind as it is, but when the acorns are falling pheasants, mallard, pigeon and jays may go to it for food. One never comes to the end of learning if one is always trying to notice all the relevant facts and to puzzle out where game is likely to be and what it will do.

Every gamekeeper wants some time off duty, and many are pressed to the limit of their endurance when pheasants are scattering in search of acorns, so it is sometimes possible for a man of good repute to help with 'walking in' the boundaries. This is the thankless task of walking round the perimeter of the estate and shooing the pheasants towards safety. No-one who wishes to learn about game should ever miss a chance of doing this, but he should leave his gun and his dog at home unless he wishes to be saddled with the sins of every poacher and hunting mongrel.

A man has ceased to be a novice at walking-up when he is seldom handicapped by having the wrong foot in front as the game rises. On good going it always pays to take the extra step which will bring the feet into a proper stance but in roots, a snipe bog or sticky ploughland it may be necessary to take special pains, such as adopting a limping gait which never brings the right foot in front of the left. Anyone too proud to do this over the last few yards to a likely flushing point will have less shooting than he might. Nevertheless, however warily a man may walk, a cock pheasant which rises close to his feet may well escape. It looks so big and the colours are so bright that it seems to be un-missable; brim-full of confidence you shoot straight at it and it flies away. Only when you realize that it is rising sharply and moving fast enough to merit a proper swing will you ruffle a single feather.

The largest version of this strolling with a gun is formal walking-up and in it every man must know his rôle and play his part. It is such a subtle matter that little can be learned from print and it is probably best for a beginner to go with an experienced pilot. A vow of silence should be taken by all hands, and the guns should keep in line with the precision of soldiers, but the rest must be learned in the field. The saying that a partridge shot while walking-up is a partridge wasted is not altogether true, although it is true that they can be mobbed to destruction. If it is done properly it can be one of the high points of the season and it calls for teamwork and a real knowledge of game.

To reduce unproductive walking our ancestors evolved shooting over pointers and setters and it is greatly to be regretted that it is hardly ever done in the lowlands of England nowadays. I have only seen it on Scottish moors myself. The essence of the business is most easily understood if we consider one man with one dog. The man walks straight forward while a setter zig-zags over a strip of ground in front of him; on locating game the dog freezes to a point and the man goes to it quickly and quietly. He pats the dog which then sneaks forward to flush the game and at this stage there may be an interesting duel between an old grouse, which knows the danger of flying, and the dog. There may be several guns, and the dogs usually work in pairs, but the overall plan is always much as described.

The man who breeds, trains and shoots over his own dogs sees the world of shooting from a very different angle from that known to one who arrives by car from some distant town and is led to his stands throughout a long day at driven game. I do not maintain that either is better than the other but only that they call for different skills and that they attract for quite different reasons. It could hardly be disputed that driven game demands more skill with the gun and calls for a higher standard of gun-fitting. Indeed the shooting of walked-up game may be comparatively easy and the fit of the gun of no great importance. The emphasis is on the knowledge of the ways of game and on teamwork, while when shooting over dogs, to some people at any rate the actual shooting is of less interest than the performance of the dogs.

The big bags are made by driving, but in one respect walking-up is harder on the game because more birds are wounded but not picked up. The reasons for this are that the ranges are longer, the birds are leaving the guns with their vulnerable parts hidden, and most walking-up takes place early in the season when the cover is thick. The remedies are good retrieving dogs, good marking of fallen birds by the men and a determination to find them, particularly the potential runners.

As walking-up involves shooting a variety of game in an unpredictable order it is wise to have general-purpose cartridges; my own preference is for number 6 shot but number 7 is probably just as good. Beginners are often too shy to ask what they are supposed to shoot at but this is a mistake. Foxes are such a pest in some hill-farming districts that failure to kill one on sight is as grievous a crime as is vulpicide in Leicestershire. Feral cats are worth asking about and the 'hare line' is important if men have to carry the game for any distance. The point is that hares are too heavy to carry far and there may be some line beyond which, by established custom, hares are not shot. A very common rule is that no ground game is shot when outward bound but that it should be killed after the party has crossed a certain line on the way home. No newcomer can be expected to know the local rules and the keeper who tells a visitor not to shoot a hare because it is too far for him, the keeper, to carry it is being neither rude nor lazy; he is just explaining a local custom.

There is a division of opinion as to whether it is better to walk upwind, across the wind or downwind when after snipe. If the wind is strong the snipe can only take off into it but it is always easier to approach from downwind. The fact that each can be right helps to keep the discussion going. If all else is equal I keep the wind in my face, but in practice you always have to double back either across the wind or down it and too much theorizing is profitless.

31

The Threshold of Formal Shooting

Most shooting men welcome a newcomer to their ranks provided that he is a safe shot and a congenial companion, but newcomers should realize that they are likely to wear out their welcome if they do not swim with the current. Let us be quite clear from the outset that this is not a case of bowing down to some sacred cow of conformity for reasons lost in the mists of antiquity, but of down-to-earth, dividend-paying efficiency. If a man is shooting entirely on his own what he does, wears or uses affects no-one but himself and he can follow his inclinations to the limit, but as soon as he joins with others he will be wise to subordinate his whims to the common good. Wise, that is, if it is important to him that he should be asked again.

Although to the lay eye an experienced shooting party may give the impression that some quaint rite, stately but useless, is being performed by dated idiots to whom the niceties of behaviour are more important than the shooting, such is far from the case. They waste neither time nor words, they keep in line to be effective, they avoid anti-social acts like shooting other people's birds, and they observe all the safety precautions meticulously. They all know the plan and they contribute to it without being specifically told to do so, and although no regimentation is to be seen they reap the rewards of perfect organization because their discipline comes from the observance of customs proved by experience to be effective. Inconspicuous clothes are worn for concealment, and unnecessary noises are avoided for the same reason, but it goes deeper than that. There is not much margin for error anywhere; success hangs on a fairly precarious thread at the best of times and anyone who fails to play his part may spoil the sport of the whole party.

Things become clearer if one thinks of a day's shooting as small-scale military manœuvres—a comparison which is by no means far-fetched—and considers how finely the balance is poised between ordered success and chaotic failure. Those more familiar with amateur theatrical productions than with military training will still recognize the necessity for having everyone there at the proper time, fully equipped and capable of fending for themselves. The old hands can prompt the recruits to some extent, but they have troubles enough of their own most of the time, and the enemy, which is the game in this case, will exploit any shortcomings to the full. Once assembled and in motion the party's main dangers spring from straggling, getting lost and somebody's failure to grasp what he is supposed to do. In practice these are closely linked because straggling brings the others in its train; it is essential that you should keep up with the guide and that you should notice his signals. For instance he will probably indicate number 3 gun's stand by holding up three fingers and pointing to a stick. If number 3 guns raises his hand in acknowledgement at once the guns are lined up quickly, neatly and in silence, but if he has to be sought out time is wasted and the wretched guide may be running like the wind to his own place when the first birds come over.

Getting lost on strange ground is embarrassingly easy but a study of a 6-inch map of the estate helps. Half the trick is to notice the direction of each walk, or drive, and to visualize one's position on the map; the other half is to keep an eye on the guide and to know what is happening.

To forget one's number was something of a crime before Hitler's war but now it seems to be less seriously regarded. Unscrupulous guns have talked the forgetful out of their right to a good stand but, whatever the ethics of that may be, it is less harmful to sport than the everlasting 'coffee-housing' which seems to have become endemic. 'Coffee-housing' is any unnecessary talk and it is the curse of the age. Although it is no more than undesirable when shooting early pheasants it is bad later in the year and it is always fatal with part-ridges and snipe. Partridges will run, literally, half a mile ahead of talking men while snipe will rise far out of range and probably leave the parish. The human voice carries unexpectedly far and wild things

Positions in which a man can sit on a shooting stick for hours without noticing the weight of his gun, although it is held perfectly safely at all times.

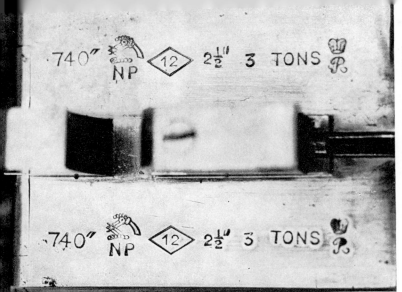

Modern proof marks.

The correct positions of the hands. Notice how the fore-finger rests on the trigger-guard to shield the triggers.

fear it. Beyond a doubt game associate whistles with human beings and it is worth knowing that the so-called 'silent' whistle is audible to game as well as to dogs.

What all this boils down to is that for the common good a shooting party should go about its business quickly, neatly and in silence. If it does this in response to hand signals and an occasional blast on a whistle it will kill more game than a coffee-housing rabble will see, or even suspect to be on the estate. No-one likes regimentation but to reach even 80% of the potential the party must deploy, manœuvre and re-form with the precision of soldiers. If the sport is to reach its zenith something of the stealth of Red Indians and the slick speed of smash and grab robbers must be added, and it is only by conforming to the accepted customs that this level can be approached.

These are the eminently sensible and practical reasons for the discipline of the shooting field, to which must, of course, be added the rules for the safe handling of guns, and a little thought shows that the common good is the only objective, while no heed is taken of tradition for its own, pompous sake.

It is however arguable whether the feeling against pump guns and automatics rests upon such perfect logic, though its existence is a fact which must be accepted. To many people such guns are oafish things which give the impression of a ruthless approach to the sport by a greedy man who is prepared to replace skill by mere weight of fire. Time may modify these opinions, but no way has yet been found to show that these guns really are unloaded when the cartridges have been taken out, and every gun must be regarded as loaded unless seen to be empty. This, to my mind, is a valid objection at present and the rest may be prejudice; but it is a powerful feeling which it would be unwise to oppose. In fact I have never seen a pump gun used against game in this country except as an experiment conducted in private.

Except that it is better not to use a 'poacher's pocket', since it is the quickest way of ruining game and clothes, I would not presume to be dogmatic about clothes; but I do think that a critical inspection of oneself in a looking-glass when returning after a long day in the rain may be revealing. Unorthodox dress, wet, muddy and covered with burrs, may create an unwanted impression and suggest a few alterations for next time; slightly old clothes of good quality hardly ever do so.

I

32

The First Formal Shoot

Most of my generation only reached the front line against driven game after an apprenticeship as a walking and general utility gun. At that time most hosts liked their guests to be in front all the time and arranged that their sons, or someone who had yet to win his spurs, should do all the subsidiary tasks. That there seemed among my father's friends to be a dearth of sons who would have filled my rôle was my good fortune, but it would have availed me nothing had I not done exactly as I was told, not only by my hosts but by the keepers also. Any beginner should seize any similar chance which comes his way and maintain, as I did, that he is lucky to be shooting at all rather than to think himself ill-used that he is not a forward gun.

However, that grounding is not always possible and I am going to launch the reader on a day at driven pheasants. He comes as my guest and I am going to give him a pilot, a retired keeper who knows the ropes, so that all the new hand has to do is to watch his front and shoot as well as may be, but with perfect safety.

He is not expected to shoot up to his true form, for everything will be new and strange, but he is expected to be sensible and quiet. A full day of driven pheasants is the culmination of a great deal of hard work for the greater part of a year; if all goes well we shall see the drives executed with the precision of military drill, all hands will be happy and rightly proud of their work. But if it is not taken seriously we may well see a particularly expensive form of exasperating chaos.

My visitor starts well by arriving twenty minutes early and properly dressed. As he draws number 2 his pilot takes him to the second stand from the right-hand end of the line for the first drive. Numbers 7 and 8 are always walking guns here while the front guns are 1 to 6; he will be number 4 at the second drive and number 6 at the third. Then he will walk as number 8 and be back at number 2 for the fifth drive. The scheme is to move up two places at each new drive thus avoiding walking twice in succession.

Arrived at his stand he fills his right-hand coat pocket with cartridges, puts his cartridge bag open on the ground, stamps a level place for his feet, loads his gun and looks about him. The neighbouring guns catch his eye and raise their hats: they are signalling that they are in position and they will not move without warning him. The pilot gives the cartridge bag a good shake to bring the brass ends uppermost so that they can be grabbed the right way round.

My guest is tense and over-anxious for he has not yet learned that it is impossible to be at maximum readiness for long and that one must relax until action calls. The wisest thing to do while waiting is a little quiet practice for the same reason that a golfer has practice swings during pauses in play. The birds will be in sight at this stand long before they are within range and the pilot points out that a scrub oak is just 40 yards to the front, so they will be in range as they top the tree.

As usual the pigeon come out first followed by blackbirds and the like and the jays are the last to leave before the pheasants. This shoot wants jays, magpies, crows and squirrels killed on sight but I forgot to say anything about it. As the first pheasant comes the guns rise from their shooting sticks and one calls softly 'Peter'. Every bird 'belongs' to the man to whom it offers the best shot and this is usually the gun over whose head it will pass; should he miss it with both barrels it then becomes anybody's and to kill it is to 'wipe the eye' of the misser.

Had my visitor noticed how Peter shot that first pheasant he would have learned an important lesson for, although it was visible for a long time before it came into range, the man stood still until it was, perhaps, 60 yards away. Then he went from his relaxed position to the 'ready', tracked the bird with eyes and muzzle for an instant (see chapter 11) and then, without hurry or delay, took it at his favourite elevation; this is a trifle flatter than 45 degrees above the horizontal for many of us. Any deviation from this routine makes things more difficult and to try to make certain of a kill by letting it come closer, correcting errors, peering or poking is to lessen the chance of a hit. Do not be slapdash, but shoot at your first choice with sober confidence just as you would write your name on an important document, for no doubt you have noticed that you produce an untypical signature if you take pains to be neat.

The pilot's calm 'Watch your front, sir' calls our man's attention back to the zone it should never have left: the frontage half-way to either neighbour. The pheasants come, and how well the novice shoots depends largely upon how much he allows his previous training to take charge. Tense muscles and anxiety prohibit even fair shooting, but as soon as the man relaxes, the fraction of training which has become subconscious, reflex action will show its worth, and just one conscious thought can be added to it. Only one, for our minds are made like that. It is a good plan to resolve to think of one thing during every shot at one drive, perhaps 'look hard at its head', and another at the next drive.

When the drive is over someone will give a signal and every gun should be unloaded, and left unloaded, until the next drive begins. Only if there is no other way of preventing the escape of a wounded bird should a shot be fired while birds are being picked up for, apart from the danger, the head of every searcher, man or dog, will jerk up and all concentration will be lost. The pilot has counted the pheasants shot by his charge and marked where they fell, so those birds are picked up quickly; had there been a runner among them he would have sent his dog for it at once.

Before long there is a call of 'forward guns this way, please' and the pilot moves briskly and silently to the guide who will take them to the next stands. In the past it was regarded as nothing short of bad manners to lag behind the guide, make the slightest noise or to forget one's number at the next drive but nowadays it is a lesser matter. Those who chatter do not realize that they are ruining their own sport, for pheasants are by no means fools, but it does discourage the men who worked hard to get the best from the day.

As a walking gun on the fourth drive my guest learns that he should not shoot at game which is going towards the forward guns and that his task is to take those going back or sideways. He will be most unpopular if he takes the high, crossing birds (crossing to him that is), which would have been oncoming shots for the forward guns if he had not interfered.

At a hot corner the pilot shows him a trick by which one gun can be made to do most of the work of a pair. The fired cartridges jump out as the man opens his gun and the pilot drops two more in. He finds that there is no need for him to take his eyes off the sky and that reloading is very quick indeed.

My guest ended the day as well as he began it; he gave the keeper the tip I suggested and ferried the beaters and keepers home in his car. He made his dog comfortable as soon as he reached his own house and he cleaned his gun before attending to himself.

Tipping keepers is a very long-standing custom, and newcomers cannot possibly know how much to give, but I have never hesitated to ask my host and, when the positions are reversed, I expect to be asked. The size of the bag affects the issue but how much honest effort was made is an important factor. In the ordinary way the one reflects the other but Lady Luck holds the top trumps and may always defeat solid merit. When that happens I should give the same tip as I should if things had gone normally but, by the same token, I should reduce my contribution if the bag was as expected despite gross mismanagement.

No matter how careful we are about shooting only those birds which are ours there are always times when two guns fire together and either might have killed it; never claim to have done so, and be content to leave the matter undiscussed.

I always make a note of how many cartridges I used during the day and how many birds which I shot were picked up, but nothing will induce me to reveal the figures to a soul. I want to know the figures so that I can eliminate faults by working on my weaknesses but I dislike the atmosphere which surrounds competitive cartridge averages. To my mind the enjoyment of shooting is not to be measured by the size of the bag, neither is the skill of a man necessarily reflected by the ratio of kills to cartridges, it being at least possible that no shot was fired at any bird which presented the slightest difficulty.

33

On Driving Pheasants

This is not for experts but for those who miss a lot of enjoyment through not knowing what to look for. Let us watch a covert of 4 acres, 280 yards by 70, driven by experts. The host has taken the forward guns inconspicuously to the downwind end while the keeper has the beaters and the walking guns well away from the wood and keeping quiet. The host's horn indicates that he is ready and the beaters move to the upwind end of the covert 'knocking in' some hedges and a patch of kale on the way. More about 'knocking in' later. The beaters spread themselves evenly across the wood, a walking gun fires into the air and the beat starts.

Tapping with sticks and covering the whole area the beaters move forward abreast of the keeper. If we could see the pheasants now we should notice that they were walking calmly away uncertain whether to hide, run away or fly. Unlike partridges they are individualists and each will decide for itself; at present they are studying the form and keeping the options open.

A few birds rise, the keeper slows the pace, the rattle of sticks increases but no voice is heard. The forward guns come into action and the pheasants must make their choice. If the beaters advance quickly they will tend to squat down and hide, they will spot gaps in the line and safe exits to the sides; if the beaters stop they will have time to consider their plan. They are most likely to fly if a beater is approaching slowly but cannot see them.

The line stops short of the main flushing points and a few men go forward putting up the birds in a steady trickle. They avoid flushing a cloud at the same instant because the guns would not have time to reload. Then the beaters move forward again beating out every particle of cover up to, and through, the final hedge. The keeper will probably swing the line so that everyone is converging on the downwind corner and getting closer together towards the end. As they come out of the wood he speaks for the first time. 'All out, sir', the host blows his horn and the drive is over; unload and pick up.

Although this looks childishly simple when it is done well it is only partly true to say that anyone can do it. Anyone can do it badly, that is the deadly thing, for the bad is the good's worst enemy. Partridges flying everywhere but over the guns ridicule the blunderer so that he mends his ways, but almost any disturbance will put a few pheasants over the guns, even though the majority may have hidden or slunk off unseen. The upshot is that those who blunder with pheasants are often not detected; they have no incentive to improve and may even pass as experts.

Now let us examine the fundamentals. The object is to send all the pheasants over the forward guns as high and as fast as possible. They cannot be driven anywhere they do not wish to go and their first choice is always to run away unseen, next best is to hide, and flying is the last resort. Then, discarding all cunning, they go flat out for a safe place. They seldom travel half a mile in the air, two hundred to four hundred yards being the usual distance, but they know that pace over the ground increases their chances of safety so they avoid flying upwind or uphill.

It follows that it is easiest to drive pheasants down a slope and down the wind to a place in which they feel safe (often the wood they regard as home) up to four hundred yards away. Remove any of these factors and the task becomes more difficult; remove enough factors and it is impossible. It is, for example, quite useless to attempt to drive a covert in the direction successfully used for generations if the sanctuary wood which attracted them has been replaced by a housing estate.

The accepted ways of getting them high into the air are to induce them to take off from ground higher than the guns or to make them fly over something tall, usually trees. Those that rise within a wood will commonly climb to clear the trees and will be higher than those which rise from the last hedge.

The whole of the foregoing, which is the basic beating and planning, might be compared to the first round of the bidding at bridge in that all subsequent brilliance is dependent upon its soundness. There are many variations of the basic strategy and some are indeed brilliant. Imagine a covert on a hillside sloping from north to south with a strong north wind blowing. Guns and beaters form a single line on the southern edge of the wood before moving north to run the pheasants into a field of kale north of the wood. The guns halt on the southern edge of the kale while the beaters go straight on, but the birds will not face the open ground beyond the kale with the wind and the slope against them. When they rise they curl back over the beaters and head for home, giving the guns good shooting.

At this point let us spare a thought for the man in charge of operations who had the nerve and confidence in his own judgment to do this. Had the wind dropped the pheasants might not have broken back; the whole lot might have gone over the hill, across the boundary and onto the land of someone who made them so welcome that they stayed where they were. A man who drove the birds out to the south could be suspected of a lack of courage but what of one who sent them east or west? There will be some curling, memorable birds among them and, though the general standard will be lower, the risk is far less. If he knows that the guns can appreciate real artistry and will forgive him if things go wrong the man in charge may well try for the highest, but if he thinks that no-one but himself will recognize his skill he may decide that a second-rate performance is all that the guns deserve.

There are usually some gathering operations before a drive. Beaters who tap along a hedge to make any pheasants there run into a wood which will be beaten out later are said to 'knock in' the hedge, while if the guns join the beaters to run the birds to some place it is called 'blanking in'. The further pheasants are run from home the more likely they are to break back.

'Stops' are anything intended to stop a pheasant running or to make it fly. They range from a piece of paper to a man with a gun. The longest artificial stop is a piece of string with rags tied to it; called 'sewelling', it is often stretched across a wood 50 yards from the end to make the pheasants rise within the wood. In such cases a man in hiding will probably twitch the string if a bird tries to walk underneath.

Whether or not pheasants are capable of logical thought they behave as if they were—within limits. Their sight and hearing are probably rather better than those of human beings; they are more observant than we are and they are much better at spotting motives. I imagine that being without speech they have to be. For instance they know at once whether another pheasant is hurrying in alarm or in pursuit of food and they react to the behaviour of other species. Like men they do foolish things when flustered but, in general, they are not stupid and it is a mistake to under-rate them because a few contribute to their own destruction.

The best way of indicating the worst faults of beating might be to report a bad drive from a pheasant's viewpoint and I very much suspect that the following would be an understatement rather than an exaggeration. 'Human noises from three hundred yards upwind alerted all members before the passage of men along one side of our wood cause some of us to leave it on the other side. Then another party approached noisily from the upwind end and walked casually through the thin undergrowth without making any determined search of thick brambles or dense cover. Their incessant chatter and loss of formation made rearward penetration of their line easy on foot and no close search was made of open areas, where many of us had squatted to try out our camouflage: of these none was detected. I regret to report that an unjustified loss of nerve caused some members to fly and suffer casualties and I submit that the human lack of a sense of smell, poor sight and worse woodcraft render flying an unwise risk.'

The vast majority of men with any length of experience of driving pheasants will go along with the views expressed so far in this chapter, but I am now going to broach a matter upon which there is a sharp difference of opinion. I happen to have been brought up in an area which believed that the use of the human voice was the negation of good beating. The rattle of tapping sticks was credited with the power of moving the pheasants along without flustering them; small boys were given clappers and the smallest shook a tin with a few pebbles in it. The man in charge of the beat was the only one who ever spoke and then only to issue essential orders, so that everyone heard and obeyed the orders. It was accepted that pheasants tended to crouch down and hide at the sound of the human voice or, at best, to panic and behave in an unpredictable manner. A quite exceptional bird would get a blast on a whistle but, by and

large, the forward guns were expected to listen for the birds' wings
and to be their own lookouts.

But I have since shot in districts where shouting by beaters is
positively encouraged; every bird which rises is greeted by cries of
'Mark!' and they are urged to leave the ground by fierce yells. To
make his orders effective the keeper must be the loudest shouter, and,
as they are repeated down the line, the total of noise is considerable.

Now I can only be sure of two results from all this shouting: first
that the beaters undoubtedly encourage themselves and enjoy it and
secondly that pheasants which were walking placidly along while
the beaters were silent react unfavourably as soon as the shouting
starts. Not only does the keeper lose control of the beaters but the
beaters lose control of the pheasants for the overpowering reason
that most of the pheasants have lost control of themselves.

To me there seems to be a strong case for working in silence but
I have never made a single convert and the closest I have ever got
to one is 'You and I know that shouting does harm and I have tried
to keep them quiet but it is hopeless. This shoot is in a shouting area
and it is no good trying to alter it.'

34

The First Partridge Drives

It is not difficult for a newcomer to grasp the elements of the art of driving pheasants, but partridges are much more complicated. The boundary of the estate is the only factor which remains constant; everything else, where the birds are likely to be, in which directions they can be driven and where they will settle, depends upon factors which are changing all the time, the chief of which are the weather and the crops in the fields. That is why your host will probably have a planning talk with the keeper before operations begin and why the plan may be altered during the day. Local knowledge is very important and experience is essential, but it is difficult to say which is the more vital. All I can say is that driving partridges is a skilled matter which demands a real knowledge of the ground to be covered, but because it takes place in the open, where one can see what is going on, a newcomer can learn the tactics quickly although the strategy can only be understood by experienced people.

One of the 'musts' is that the guns should get into place quickly and without talking while another is that, at their stands, they must be reasonably well concealed. If the hedges are tall and ragged the guns can be far enough back from the cover to allow them to shoot the birds in front, but one of the curses of our times is that hedges are often cut so low that the guns must be almost touching the twigs if they are to remain concealed. Then the coveys may be upon them so quickly that shooting to the front is all but impossible and the guns must turn and take them as going-away birds, which is generally regarded as distinctly second best.

So let us consider the better part first and imagine that we are some yards back from an overgrown hedge with our fellow guns ranged in a straight line on either side of us. The zones in which safety allows us to shoot are shown in figure 11: a covey which comes between two guns may be fired at by either but each should take the birds on his own side of the covey and only when they are within his own zone. What you must never, never do is to follow through from your forward zone to the rear with your gun at a flat angle. Strictly speaking you are allowed to shoot to any point of the compass if your gun is at a really steep angle but for a novice to do so would be asking for trouble. Even an experienced man shooting among strangers would be wise to drop the butt as soon as he had traversed to within forty-five degrees of the line of guns and to turn with the barrels pointing vertically upwards. The absolute prohibition placed upon swinging a gun through the line by our ancestors, whether the gun were fired or not, has survived to this day; they qualified it by allowing the gun to be fired right down the line if it were steeper than forty-five degrees above the horizontal but nowadays it is wiser not to insist on your rights.

When shooting to the front it must never be forgotten that the

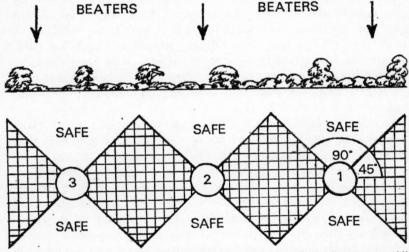

Figure 11. The safe and dangerous zones when shooting driven game. All the angles are forty-five degrees or ninety degrees, the guns are numbered and the danger zones are shaded. The beaters behind the hedge must not be forgotten.

beaters are behind the hedge: wise men have decreed that no gun should be fired to the front at an angle of less than forty-five degrees above the horizontal and, though this may be more cautious than is really necessary, no novice who obeyed the rule could be faulted. If a hare comes it should always be allowed to pass through the line before being shot.

This diversion about safe zones of fire has distracted attention from our stand thirty yards back from a nice big hedge where we were waiting for the first birds of the day to be driven over us. The delights of this wait have been described in graphic prose by some well-known writers, but if I let my attention wander to the clustering towers of William of Wykeham, or to a string of the best blood in England returning from their morning gallop, I should not expect to shoot very well. The point is that partridges may arrive unannounced, at speed and taking evasive action. It is true that they fly more slowly than pheasants, and if they held their course and gave warning of their coming they would be relatively easy to hit, but in practice the difficulty is always to see the birds early enough to do what one knows one should and to counter their swerves. Most novices try to cope with this shortage of time by being right on their toes, keyed up and poised for action at all times, but they are entirely wrong and they are defeating themselves. No-one can maintain a state of instant readiness for long; to attempt to do so must result in rigidity and slowness, and the proper course is to go to the other extreme. One should relax with the gun held lightly and the weight balanced comfortably on both feet.

Should you hear the keeper's whistle, a whirr of wings or a partridge's alarm call, do *not* grip the gun more tightly and stiffen to attention but move calmly to the 'ready' position and keep as relaxed as you can. Ignore everything outside your own zone but when you see a bird glue your eyes to it and shoot at once. Do not hurry, or pause to make certain of a kill, but mount the gun with a stout heart and shoot in the tempo you have learned while shooting oncoming clays. As the partridge crumples into a ball of feathers fix your eyes on another and swing smoothly, coolly but resolutely, paying no attention whatever to anything else.

To let the birds get close is to make things more difficult. The crack shots kill them twenty-five to thirty yards in front, which means that they first move when the range is considerably longer, but whenever circumstances permit these experts take them far out in front, probably at forty-five yards or so. Though this is seldom possible it is fundamental that the first shot should be fired as soon as maybe, provided that accuracy is not sacrificed to haste.

A good deal of confidence must be generated before one can slide the gun up and shoot at the first glimpse of a partridge but to pause, or to move with anything less than full determination, is to ensure a miss. So much for what we ought to do but all too often the first hint a novice has of partridges in the vicinity is the sight of a covey bursting like a star shell, left, overhead and right, as they clear the hedge in front of him. It is more than startling, it is unnerving, and the usual result is a frozen pause followed by two ill-directed shots. How, then, are we to do in the time available what we know perfectly well we should do?

Well, every truthful man will admit that he has been struck motionless by the sudden appearance of a covey at close quarters, but it should not happen at all. For one thing if a man is relaxed but alert he will go into action on the reflex, as opposed to freezing, and if he has trained himself properly he will keep his eye on the first bird he saw and he will not be distracted by the others. More important, if he had been watching his own front to the exclusion of all else he would have seen the partridges before they saw him.

Wearing out your eyes and nerves by peering here, there and everywhere a partridge might manifest itself is worse than useless. In *Game Shooting* Churchill advises that the man should gaze 'steadily into the "blue" at the approximate point in the air, not where he thinks the birds might appear, but where he would like to kill them if they do'. This is advice from the fountain head indeed but Churchill was a fast shot as well as a very good one. I try to give myself a little more time by gazing at the point where, should partridges appear, I shall start to mount my gun. Then they come into view without surprising me and I react normally. In point of fact you can see most of your own front without turning your head and very few partridges can sneak up unseen.

Before leaving the subject of shooting quickly at low oncomers I should like to anticipate perfectly fair questions about how it is possible to incorporate all the routine about pointing the gun at the bird with the hands, tracking it with eyes and muzzle, dabbing a straight left onto its face and swinging up the smoke trail. Great stress was laid on the importance of practising these things and yet it is manifestly impossible even to think of them in the time available. That is perfectly true, conscious thought of the component parts is not possible, but they must be there if the whole is to work. For example, when a fast bowler sends a half-volley at a batsman's off stump does the latter think about his foot going to the pitch of the ball, of playing down the line and of sending the bat right through? Surely not; he recognizes the half-volley, keeps his eye on it and lets training look after the component parts. That is what you should do with shooting, and if you have trained enough all the bits will be present and the whole will work as intended.

Shooting partridges after a covey has passed overhead is chiefly a matter of turning round quickly, with the barrels vertical, without losing your balance and, preferably, without taking your eyes off the bird you intend to shoot. If you take the precaution of making a level place to stand on as soon as you reach your marker you will turn as well as the time you have devoted to learning footwork deserves if, but only if, you are wearing suitable boots. The shot is usually at going-away birds low down and not the most difficult if you have time to settle comfortably and take it before the birds have gone far. There is a school of thought which seldom shoots at birds in front but picks up the line as the covey approaches, turns in plenty of time and has two shots as the birds leave the gun. Certainly they have some success but I withhold admiration; I greatly prefer to see driven game killed in front and, without a shred of logic to support me, I regard the method as that of defeatists, poor-spirited and generally second best. But I do not censure a man who honestly shoots within his own limitations and strives for no more than a stylish kill in front, a good turn and a neat shot behind. That is the high road to improvement and one which is the logical step for a beginner to take.

Sometimes the guns are placed so close to the screening hedge that most of the shooting must be done at going-away birds and, to avoid this, hides can be made either of hurdles or of bales of straw. These hides can provide perfect cover but sometimes the weather changes so that the intended drives cannot be made and the kindest host can do no more than put his guests close to an inadequate hedge and watch his treasured partridges shot from behind. Incidentally, in partridge shooting hides are more often called screens but the word 'butts' seems to be creeping in from grouse shooting; all these terms have the same meaning but some shooting men are careful about such details.

Occasionally, either because the partridges have been driven over a belt of trees or because the guns are in a depression of some kind, the birds are presented more like driven pheasants. These are almost the only conditions in which there is plenty of time to shoot driven partridges in front; the technique is that used against driven pheasants except that partridges will usually descend after crossing an obstacle instead of carrying on at the same height as pheasants normally do.

However the coveys come you must always select the bird you intend to shoot and keep your eyes glued to it alone. If you change your mind and go for another bird you will probably miss, and if you are in too much of a hurry when thinking of a right and left you will miss the first shot. The tendency is to start for the second bird just before, instead of just after, firing the first barrel. Do not be over-eager to get rights and lefts. Concentrate first on firing the first shot without haste or hesitation and then go smoothly with the second barrel. Your feet have as much to do with the accuracy of the second shot as anything else and when you have taught them to move as they should without conscious thought you will kill with the second barrel surprisingly easily.

It is best to warm up slowly, and I always do a little quiet practice with my swing and footwork on reaching my first stand. If the advance is led by a few solitary red-legs I am grateful because my chief concern is to get the feel of shooting accurately rather than quickly. Only when I feel that normal running temperatures, as it were, have been reached do I really set about getting a right and left. Most novices would be wise to do something of the sort and to shoot a few clays before leaving home if this is possible.

An extension of this is my feeling that people should hesitate to go out with a pair of guns until they can kill two birds in front fairly consistently. The problems of handling two guns with a loader are discussed later, but it is the mental state caused by having the increased firepower available which concerns us now. It is true that to be worried about missing induces bad shooting, and that a man with only one barrel is often over-careful, but to have four barrels at hand is to go to the other extreme. The measure of deliberation which is essential to accuracy tends to disappear and the discharge

The Premiere, £1,725 plus tax.

The Hercules, £690 plus tax.

The Regal, £400 plus tax.

A vivid demonstration that the hands alone can align a gun correctly. Surprisingly, the method calls for no more skill than is given to most of us, but no novice should attempt to use it. Photograph by kind permission of G. T. Garwood Esq.

of all four barrels seems to be regarded as a bounden duty, although it is nothing of the kind. It may not be realized that it takes a good man to get off three reasonably accurate shots at one covey and that many of us would shoot better, and enjoy our shooting more, if we were a trifle more deliberate and only went for the second gun when Fortune was being very kind.

Whenever only one gun is being used it is not essential to have anyone with you at the stand, but it is a great help if a *trained* man is there to mark and count the fallen birds. He will not get in your way but he can watch the birds right down to the ground while you look for another unless the first barrel produced an obvious potential runner. You are supposed to count the birds as you shoot them and to know their approximate locations at the end of the drive. I record them on a mental cricket field, one to long leg, one to third man and two at cover point perhaps. Other people do it on the face of an imaginary clock.

The man I should really like to have behind me at a hot corner is an instructor from a shooting school where I had been practising. These men can always make me shoot better than my true form and they can be induced, at a price, to spend the whole day coaching you while you are shooting game.

An untrained companion who distracts you is a nuisance; one who finds the weather oppressive and removes an inconspicuous coat to expose a brightly coloured pullover discourages the approach of game as effectively as the companion who will not keep still; but the man I will not tolerate at any price is he who sucks his teeth in lofty contempt when I miss. I ought to be sufficiently detached to say that the opinion of such an ignoramus is of no consequence, perhaps I should have the courage to thrust my gun into his hands and invite him to do better, but I have never done more than take the coward's way out by shedding him when opportunity offered. If famous batsmen can lose their wickets to bad balls while leading jockeys are thrown at the start and great golfers miss tiny putts in the Open then, dammit, I should be allowed to miss my full share without being put upon.

To shoot into the thick of a covey, instead of picking an individual bird, is called 'browning' and it is an offence for a variety of reasons, one of which is that we go shooting, in part at any rate, to do something difficult as well as we can, not to shed oceans of blood. If you

K

ever sink so low as to do this on purpose (accidental 'browns' can happen), I hope that you get your just reward—a clean miss with both barrels. You will understand why this is probable if you study a photograph of a covey in flight for, although in the heat of action the sky seems to be covered by birds, the photo will show that there is much more blank sky than there is of partridge. Even if the two birds you have in mind for a right and left are flying close together you must concentrate on one if you are not to shoot between them and hit neither.

Four partridges shot from one covey by one man can be compared to a round of golf in par or to a break of something like a hundred at snooker, that is to say it is a very difficult thing to do, even though the basic plan is no more than two in front, change guns, turn and take two behind. But let us dream of the heights: it is said that the only way to shoot five partridges from the same covey is to shoot one far in front, change guns, then two more in front, change again, turn and kill two behind. I have fired the five rounds but never have I killed with all of them. Good luck to you if you ever make the attempt; I hope that you do better than I, but if you bring it off do remember that the loader played a big part.

35

A Tourist amongst Grouse

The turn of Fortune's wheel which allowed me to shoot large numbers of snipe abroad enabled me to write about them with confidence but it also ensured that I was over forty years old before I first saw grouse driven over guns. I therefore approach this chapter with the greatest diffidence in the full knowledge that many novices are better informed than I am and that I can do no more than record a tourist's impressions.

That being so I have compiled the bulk of what follows from a diary I kept during my first grouse shooting holiday, excluding as far as possible all impressions and knowledge gained on subsequent visits to the moors. I have no wish to turn a book of instruction into an autobiography, but my hope is that an accurate description of one beginner's experiences may be of value to others.

As I travelled north I knew full well that I was a raw novice who might well make himself look very, very foolish indeed but that I could count upon a few solid assets. I was a beginner at grouse but I could hold my own against lowland game and, as I had just finished a full shooting season in an outpost of what we used to call the Empire, I was in full practice. Moreover, in view of trials by grouse to come, I had spent some time at a shooting school on returning to England. As far as training off the course was possible I was as well prepared as I could be and my host had told me what clothes I should need.

My first difficulty was something I had neither heard of nor suspected: the light was different and I could not judge distances. For the first twenty-four hours in Banff I genuinely did not know whether

147

an object was forty or twenty yards away; this wore off by the third day but I have since learned that others have had the same experience.

The month was September and we spent the first few days on relatively low ground with partridges as the main objective, but a few grouse were included. I shot well enough against the partridges but I reacted lethargically to the grouse. Due to the fact that I did not recognize a grouse until I had had a good look at it I ignited slowly and then, pressed for time, shot badly.

My first impression of a line of butts was that the whole lay-out was highly dangerous, the more so since the entrances were at the sides. The line curved over the moor but it also rose and fell so that I, in the middle, was ideally placed to shoot into all the other butts. Had I wished to change sides and assist the grouse I could not have selected a better place from which to pour covering fire upon the guns. My safe zones were not the comfortable arcs of ninety degrees which we have when driving partridges but tiny cones of about thirty degrees. There were safety sticks on either side to guide me and to prevent following through without raising the muzzle, but I should have felt less of a menace to my neighbours and more secure myself had there been solid screens of sheet iron on either side of my butt.

The view from that first butt was wonderful; it was a very clear day and I could see right across the Firth to Orkney behind me, but without distinctive features on the moor to my front I found it curiously difficult to keep my bearings and to remember the boundaries of my own forward zone.

It was also difficult to pick out approaching coveys and to estimate the speed of their coming. I realized that this was due to my lack of experience in these new conditions. When I hear a pheasant's wings I know more or less where it is and where, and when, I hope to shoot it even if the bird is out of sight, but I had no background knowledge of grouse and it reduced my effectiveness.

When Duncan was in my butt he loaded for me and did most of the thinking, and then I shot reasonably well provided that I was not too ambitious. The ordinary techniques of shooting which I have described in this book held good and if I could concentrate on the shooting the results were satisfactory. But when I was alone the strange surroundings, the nagging knowledge that I could easily pepper someone and, above all, my lack of familiarity with grouse and the moors caused a sharp drop in the standard of my shooting.

My host stressed that if you stand perfectly still in the butt your silhouette will not turn grouse but that if you move they will take effective evasive action. The pace of the birds over the ground varied enormously, as they seemed to be prepared to face much stronger winds than partridges will. In the ordinary way things had to be somewhat in my favour if I was to take one in front and one behind without pressing; when they came down a strongish wind I had to see the bird well in front if I was to fire before it was over the butts, but when they had the wind in their faces there was ample time to shoot two in front as they hung in the wind.

Most of the drives were preceded by a longish walk uphill to the butts. This was often through deep heather and that contradiction in terms a precipitous swamp; had I not been fairly fit at the time exhaustion would have been an added problem. Once arrived at the butt there was always a long wait as the beaters brought in a great sweep of moorland and it was all too easy to allow tension to build up as I searched and peered for grouse which did not come. Muscular tension alone prohibits even fair shooting but I fancy that one's eyes slow down as well, because after a long, eye-straining vigil an empty sky would suddenly be filled with grouse at close quarters.

Duncan was an expert at judging when we should man the defences and we usually spent the waiting time making ourselves comfortable and improving the floor of the butt. This proved to be a good way of avoiding tension while doing something useful, as I cannot shoot properly when either stumbling about on rounded cobblestones or ankle deep in mud.

Between the driving days we walked up both grouse and partridges and I took to it readily enough as soon as I learned to react quickly to rising grouse. They usually gave going-away shots with no special features.

In the light of later knowledge I now make provision for entertainment on the days when rain and gales make shooting impossible and I take particular care to have clothes and boots in which I can walk a long way. I also take pains to be in good practice with my gun and in reasonable physical condition before I leave for the moors.

The charge that I was unduly dependent upon Duncan may be well-founded but the fact remains that he, born and bred upon the moors, had a store of grouse knowledge in his bones which no new-comer could approach. In other shooting fields I have seen men who were distinctly useful shots at English game perform like novices when first encountering different game in strange surroundings and I expected that the same would be true of me. I agree that it would be better to have enough knowledge of grouse to enable one to stand on one's own feet, and each year I get closer to that point, but until I reach it I expect to shoot less well at grouse than upon my home ground. Whether I got on faster by taking advice from a well-informed loader than I should have done by trying to go it alone may be open to question, but I certainly enjoyed the shooting more when he guided me.

36

Teamwork with a Loader

There is not so much shooting with pairs of guns as there used to be but if you ever have a loader with whom you can practise for a period of time you should adopt the drill set out in detail in Churchill's book *Game Shooting;* not only is it an excellent method in my opinion, but because it is in print, all hands can learn the same drill without debate. It is the fastest method which I have encountered but it must be done reasonably well if it is to be safe, and other routines are sometimes favoured on the grounds that they can be done badly with less risk. Whatever method you select you should practise with the loader in slow time and go slowly and carefully in the field. You have probably noticed that true novices seldom have accidents in cars but that the man who has just ceased to be a novice often has a bump.

The besetting danger is that the barrels of the two guns will be knocked together and dented, indeed this is the commonest result of excitement or over-confidence.

I like to have a hand guard on my gun to protect my left hand from the chill of the barrels on a cold morning or their heat during hectic shooting but I never use one with a loader. The point is that the handguard may slip when the barrels are vertical and the gun is supported by the left hand only (a situation which only arises with a loader), with results which are too horrible to think about.

A loader will often count and mark the birds for you, sometimes there are local customs which involve the gun saying 'hit' or 'miss' after each shot, and sometimes the loader knows how the birds are likely to fly at each stand and helps you enormously. If, as sometimes happens, the loader can genuinely see the shot in the air he may coach you into shooting really well, but there have been loaders whose claims to be able to see shot were not well-founded. Generally they are towers of strength, friendly, helpful and genuinely keen that you should have a good day; for my part I always want both gun and loader to enjoy the day and to be able to take pride in a high level of attainment reached in a pleasant atmosphere. Very seldom does one encounter the loader who sets the tone of the day by remarking that things were different when he loaded some vast number of cartridges for the famous Mr X, when the same vast number of birds were picked up, while looking critically at one's gun. If such a fate overtook me, and it never has although I have heard of it, I should be inclined to make a tactful approach for a rearrangement among the loaders.

37

Miscellanea

Sitting shots

Everyone who reads shooting magazines must have noticed how frequently the question of how one should shoot a sitting target is raised, and the question astonishes me only slightly less than the variety of the advice which is tendered in reply. From childhood to this day if I have wanted to hit a stationary object I have always treated my gun exactly as if it were a rifle. That is to say I habitually tuck my head down onto the stock, close my left eye, line the centre of the standing breech and the foresight onto the target and squeeze the trigger.

I know that this will centre the pattern onto the bull because I try my guns' patterns on plates; if it did not do so I should aim off in accordance with the evidence of those plates.

Since any white-washed wall or large sheet of paper will serve as a plate and provide the correct answer beyond possibility of doubt those who seek advice through journals lack a realistic approach. But when I read that one should shoot so many inches, or feet, below a sitting pigeon, at the reflection of a duck on the water or at the turf below a hare I feel that fantasy is taking over from ballistics. Trial alone can find out where any particular firearm shoots and I find it difficult to believe that anyone could suppose otherwise.

Snipe

The comparative rarity of snipe in this country and the fact that their jinks are almost unpredictable have combined to produce a belief that special methods must be used to shoot them.

In fact the problems would seem to be those of degree rather than of kind, and although some of the ordinary skills must be sharpened nothing new is required. Specifically one must start very early, point the gun at the bird with the hands, track it with eyes and muzzle during the whole process of mounting and fire at one's first choice. Although all these are desirable when shooting at any moving object, snipe demand them in full measure. An occasional bird may need a swing as swift as that needed for a crossing teal but very little is usually required and they are knocked out by a light blow.

With practice your whole body, and especially your hands, will follow the course and tempo of the snipe much as a rider maintains an even tension on the reins of a galloping horse. You will tend to follow a jink but if it comes at exactly the wrong moment you will probably miss and that risk must be accepted. Jinks should not cause undue alarm, for every one keeps the snipe within range for a little more time.

It is not essential to fire before the butt reaches the shoulder but to know that you can do so gives confidence. You will not feel the recoil if the gun is grasped firmly. In a previous chapter I have said that an experienced man reacts to the 'scaarp'; he points his gun towards the sound and starts mounting it so that the gun is part of the way up and he is poised to shoot by the time he sees the bird. The time so gained is all-important and the snipe is often killed before it can jink.

In connection with pointing the barrels with the hands while mounting the gun, I once made a series of experiments in connection with firing the ·303 service rifle both from the hip and while going through the motions of bayonet fighting. One of the things I noticed was that if one fired as one lunged, both the bullet and the point of the bayonet hit the same place which was always close to the spot upon which one's eyes were fixed. I have never had cause to doubt that I correctly concluded that the hands can point a barrel with considerable accuracy without the aid of conventional aiming.

Woodcock

'Cock do not fly very fast or very high and they are relatively easy to hit when they are out in the open, but the vast majority are seen, or rather half-seen, in woods or among bushes and scrub. There they demonstrate their complete mastery of the art of controlled flying as they weave and bank between the trunks on wings which make no sound. There is a ghostly quality about their flight, as there is about the flight of owls, which may be why both are associated with witchcraft. Unlike snipe they rise in silence and one usually has no more than a series of glimpses of an oddly shaped, brown bird dodging between the trees in silence.

But the effect of a call of 'Woodcock' on a shooting party is always electrifying and is often alarming; some special aura seems to be attached to 'cock which results in men shooting much closer to their fellow human beings than they would otherwise dream of doing. They are certainly good eating, a trifle unusual, and their pin feathers are esteemed as trophies, but this is not an adequate explanation of the fact that someone takes a chance which he should not have done for every two or three woodcock which are killed.

In my view woodcock are really a bit of a joke; they are good fun but they have a false reputation which does not justify all the fuss. They are not even difficult when out in the open and Lady Luck holds all the top trumps when they are among trees. There the best of shots can only act as opportunity permits and there is no golden route to success. If an orthodox swing seems to offer the best chance I hope that no timber will shelter the bird at the critical instant and ignore the trees while swinging, but if a better chance is offered by waiting until the 'cock crosses a certain clear patch I just wait and either swing or snap as judgment says is proper; for me, at any rate, no good ever comes from dwelling on the trigger while hoping for an unobstructed view of muzzle and bird separated by the correct angle. The best of shots may be defeated by an unconsidered bough and the bird may jink into a pattern of shot which was thoroughly ill-directed, so it is best to regard wood-cock as an entertaining lottery.

Wildfowl

Traditionally wildfowl are associated with big guns throwing heavy loads of large shot from long, heavily-choked barrels and it is quite true that such a gun may serve your purpose better than any other. You would be wise however to think to the end of the matter before you buy one because they are highly specialized things whose usefulness is strictly limited.

It cannot be disputed that by balancing a load of shot and the size of the pellets against the bore, choke and weight of the gun a weapon which will outrange an ordinary 12-bore game gun can be produced, but it does not follow that it will always out-shoot it. Let us suppose that a 10-bore weighing nine pounds outranges a 12-bore weighing six and a half pounds by ten yards, which may not be far from the truth—that ten yards of extra range is only useful when the target is either out of the 12-bore's range or when there is ample time to bring the big gun into action, for on all other occasions the handling qualities of the smaller gun will let you bring it into use so much sooner.

If you were in hiding and saw duck flighting in from the sea for a minute or so before they passed overhead the 10-bore, with its extra range, might well be more effective, but if darkness or any other circumstance places the emphasis on quick handling within a 12-bore's range the smaller gun will kill more game. The same is even more true of 8-bores, and the point is that although the big bores undoubtedly rule one part of the roost they can play no other rôle.

The chapter on choosing a gun for game, chapter 21, describes some of the alternatives which are open to a man who can own only one gun, but it has to be accepted that no one gun is ideal for all the different kinds of shooting.

Wildfowling calls for heavy clothes as well as heavy guns and it is very easy to reduce your shooting performance either by wearing too much above the waist or by having too much gun for your strength. Let us suppose that you have been exposed for hours to sleet driven by a freezing wind in the mud and discomfort of a gulley on the foreshore and that at last some duck are heading to-wards you. All your knowledgeable planning and spartan endurance will count for nothing if you do not mount and swing your gun reasonably well, and to do this it is essential to have freedom of movement from the waist up and to maintain the fit of the gun. Clothes which are thin at the front of the right shoulder but thick and warm elsewhere are invaluable, and they can be contrived by resourceful men or by their wives. If even one jersey and an anorak are added to normal clothing on the right shoulder the stock feels too long and the man tends to lower his head to the stock instead of raising the comb to his cheek, with disastrous effects on his shooting. Too heavy a gun has the same effect and I mention this at this point because shortening the stock is helpful in both cases. A one-gun man can do something by having a thick horn plate on the butt for normal shooting and a thin one for use with extra clothing, while a man who has a special, heavy gun for wildfowling would be wise to have the stock anything up to one inch shorter than that of his normal game gun. This is partly to allow for extra clothing and partly because a heavier gun calls for a shorter stock.

If a man can be induced to practise mounting and swinging his gun while wearing his foreshore clothes in front of a looking-glass he can check any tendency to duck down onto the stock as he prac- tises swinging as freely as he can while sitting and kneeling. Hides for both wildfowl and pigeon are often made for maximum concealment but without provision for a free swing through a big arc both hori- zontally and vertically. If the birds come into one small part of the sky this may not be important but it is galling in the extreme to wait for hours and then have opportunities to shoot which cannot be taken because the hide prevents one getting at the birds.

Pigeon

If you do not shoot pigeon you are missing a lot of good sport and some of the most testing shooting which exists in this country. Un- like driven pheasants, where at a good stand you can take bird after bird in much the same place in the sky with very much the same swing, pigeon call for every shot in your repertoire in an unpredict- able order and demand that you should be well hidden and as still as a statue until the very last moment.

Some good books have been published about pigeon shooting and they provide the basic knowledge about flight lines, decoys, the making of hides and how to get within range of the pigeon in general. Without that knowledge there will be a lot of waiting for little shoot- ing, but it is outside the scope of this book which is concerned more with the skilful handling of the gun and the novice's first steps in the shooting field. For this reason I do not want to do more than to repeat the maxim that time spent in reconnaissance is seldom, if ever, wasted.

I am probably in the minority in thinking that the greatest enjoy- ment comes from shooting pigeon which are in full flight, travelling from one place to another, while standing in a hide which allows me to use my feet to the full. As a consequence I have to make a more elaborate hide than is usual and to accept that comparatively few pigeon will come within range. My cartridge average, the ratio of kills to fired cartridges, may be notably low in those conditions but the shooting is memorable.

The highest cartridge average can be made by killing them while they are roosting or feeding on the ground, and the big bags are made by shooting over decoys, but for the sheer joy of taking on a pigeon which is doing its best in circumstances which do not put me at a disadvantage I place at the top of the list the shooting by a man standing normally of pigeon which are making a passage. Nevertheless shooting over decoys can be very good fun if the hide can be made so that the man is not too cramped. Excellent hides can be made from bales of straw or camouflaged hurdles but the disadvantage of all hides built on the surface is that the man must do most of his shooting from a sitting position. The best hide I ever had was a camouflaged hole in a field of kale which allowed me to stand up while shooting over decoys and many people would think that this approached the ideal.

The ordinary techniques of shooting hold good, but birds dropping in to land by decoys call for the realization that they are descending sharply while moving forward at a deceptive pace. Pigeon have very good eyes, and although they may not see a man who is reasonably well hidden if he keeps perfectly still they will detect movement at once and take very effective evasive action. In theory one should stand perfectly still in the 'ready' position until one slides the butt up and kills the pigeon before it can swerve, but it is a difficult thing to do in practice. To conceal the inevitable movement of the barrels some people coat them with discoloured white-wash because it can be wiped off easily afterwards.

Pigeon are certainly a test of accurate shooting but they are not as resistant to shot as is commonly supposed. They often fly on after losing a cloud of feathers but their bodies are very much smaller than their feathered outline and one doubts if the body is struck as often as appears probable. Also many people habitually shoot at them when they are really out of range. I always use an ordinary game gun with more or less standard loads of shot no larger than number 5 but some men whose opinion I respect swear by long cases and heavy loads.

38

Range and the Vulnerability of Game

Although it is often said that the maximum range of a 12-bore is forty yards with the right barrel and fifty yards with the left, beginners should not shoot at more than forty with either as the risk of wounding is too great. Here I am writing of the maximum sporting range, at which either a clean kill or a complete miss is to be expected, for any shotgun is dangerous at far greater distances.

However, it is not enough to convince people that forty yards is a sensible maximum range because most of us are poor judges of distance along the ground and downright bad where heights are concerned. Though they may be players of bowls who can judge the distance of the jack to a fraction, or golfers who can chip to within a yard or two, when it comes to estimating the range to game they will probably be at least one-third of the distance wrong. It is only a matter of training and anyone can learn by measuring the distance and taking a careful note of what the different species look like at maximum range. If one counts, say, forty-two steps from a drinking trough in a breeding pen one can really memorize what pheasants look like at that distance: notice how big they seem, the brightness of the colours and how clearly you see the outline of the head. The same thing can be done with wildfowl near an ornamental lake and with pigeon in the garden. Can you see a rabbit's eye at forty yards?

Heights are more difficult to learn because we have so few known heights to guide us but it should be remembered that a big oak tree is seldom fifteen yards high and often only twelve. Many people will not believe this until they measure the length of their own shadow and that of a tall tree and do the sum. Pheasants usually rise to clear the trees and then fly more or less level, so they are probably less than twenty yards away as they pass overhead if the ground is level; even if they are shot with the gun at an angle of forty-five degrees above the horizontal the range will be only twenty-eight yards. Yet pheasants thirty yards up will bring general admiration and those thirty-five yards high will be adjudged right out of range. They are certainly difficult to hit but if the man goes for them with a stout heart and a cool head he will kill his share for they are in fact well within range. Broadly speaking pheasants are only too high when they take off high up on one hill and fly to another over a gun in a valley. Wildfowl are often too high, but if it is remembered that a mallard is smaller than a pheasant fewer mistakes will be made. The appear-ance of pigeon at different heights can be learned in most towns from the fact that each floor of a modern block of flats adds about 10 feet to the height.

After killing an oncoming bird it is a good plan to look for feathers floating in the air. If the first barrel is fired when the bird is forty-two yards away it will be forty yards from the gun when it meets the shot, yet the floating feathers show that most of us take them much later than that, often at twenty-five yards or less, and then we have to hurry with the second barrel!

It is often said in all seriousness that the feathers of ducks and geese are so dense that it is better to let them pass and to shoot from behind so that the pellets can travel up the feathers more easily. Does this advantage really outweigh the fact that the bird is 'riding the punch', and why should any thinking person shoot at the body when the long, vulnerable neck and head are visible? The patterns of all shot no larger than number 4 are so dense that one centred on the head will probably hit the head or neck, where one pellet may kill outright and two make a near certainty, and the edge of the pattern will catch the body. Certainly one will sometimes fail to centre the pattern on the head, but surely the first step towards a clean kill is to shoot at the most vulnerable place and let the law of averages work in one's favour.

Although ducks and geese are sturdy birds which fly strongly, they are often knocked out by a relatively light blow which one would expect to leave a pheasant with the ability to run. Indeed any pheasant which falls with its head held up should be treated as a potential runner even if it hits the ground with a tremendous thump.

It may bounce and lie motionless for a minute or so only to recover and prove to be a strong runner with all its wits about it. The remarkable intelligence shown by pheasants which have only a few moments before suffered the two shocks of being shot down and hitting the ground with pulverizing force never ceases to astonish me. Snipe are such specialized fliers that they are often put right out of action by a single pellet while woodpigeon have a reputation for toughness which may not be altogether justified.

Even so it is worth keeping an eye on a pigeon, or any other bird, which one thinks was hit even though it showed no signs of damage; the reaction to shot is sometimes delayed and the bird may fly a quarter of a mile, or more, before either 'towering' or falling normally. A 'towered' bird is always dead when it reaches the ground and it usually drowns in its own blood after damage to its lungs. I am prepared to believe that 'towering' can be caused by a blow on the skull, but I have never recovered a 'towered' bird which did not have a lot of blood in its beak and nostrils.

Quite experienced men are sometimes deceived into believing that they have wounded a bird by a curious flicker in its flight immediately after the gun was fired. Until learned men told me that this is connected with a sonic boom, the speed of shot being close to that of sound, I thought that the flick in the flight was caused by the air disturbed by the passing shot. Once the jerk in the flight has been correctly identified the mistake will not be repeated, because it resembles nothing else.

Wounding a hare is very distressing and I hate to see them shot at more than thirty-five yards or so. From the side they are very vulnerable, and can be killed outright at forty-five yards, but from the rear the rump hides all the vitals except the back of the neck with its distinctive patch of russet fur. That is all you have to go for and the best chance is to shoot between the tips of her ears, as you will almost certainly kill her cleanly or miss her altogether.

Subject to reservations, all wounded things should be fired at no matter how great the range may be, and it is sometimes possible to fluke a hit, and end the misery, at eighty yards or more. This fact brings home most forcibly that the lethal range of our guns is far greater than the sporting ranges but a sense of proportion must be maintained. If the ground may be swept by irresponsible fire no man dare send a dog for a runner or go himself, and it should be recog-

L

nized that good dogs and good pickers-up are the great curtailers of suffering. I have always admired the back gun who fielded some of the shot intended to dispatch a running pheasant and called in beautifully modulated tones : 'James, if you hit me below the belt again I shall be compelled to return your fire.'

To end the chapter, it sometimes happens that a number of pellets get stuck together during their passage up the barrel. This should not happen but it does, and the result is that a queerly-shaped lump of lead leaves the muzzle at the standard velocity but much better equipped to overcome the resistance of the air than are single pellets. The flight of such mis-shapen projectiles is unpredictable, but they are probably responsible for the windows which are broken at distances of four hundred yards or the like and also for the kills which are undoubtedly made occasionally at quite enormous distances. This fusing of several pellets is called 'balling'; its existence is recognized but not much is known about the ultimate range of the 'balls'.

A Glossary of Some Shooting Terms

Aim	To direct a firearm by aligning the sights onto the target as a rifleman does. To do this with a moving shotgun is a bad fault.
Aim off	To aim at some point other than the target which it is intended to hit in order to compensate for a known fault of the weapon or for some outside influence such as the wind.
Automatic	A type of single-barrelled shotgun from which a fired cartridge is ejected mechanically and a live round is carried automatically from magazine to chamber. All such guns are operated either by gas from the fired cartridge or by recoil.
Bag	The game shot and picked up during a day's shooting.
Balling	Shot are said to ball when a number of pellets are fused together during their passage through the barrel.
Beat	A subdivision of a shoot, often in the charge of an under-keeper, hence beat-keeper as distinct from head keeper.
Beater	One who flushes game so that it may be shot.
Beater's gun	A man with a gun who walks with the beaters in order to shoot game which breaks back. A **beater's gun who shoots game going towards the forward guns is likely to incur their displeasure.** Also called a *walking gun*.
Blanking or *blanking-in*	If beaters go through an area with the intention of moving game from it to ground whence it will be flushed later they are said to blank, or to blank-in, that area.

Bore

Or gauge. The old smooth-bore muskets were described as of 12-bore if the diameter of the barrels made them suitable for the use of spherical lead balls of which 12 weighed one pound. A 16-bore fired balls each weighing one sixteenth of a pound, and so on. This description has lingered into our era but it does not mean that such balls may be fired by a modern gun with safety; indeed it would be highly dangerous if the barrel had any amount of choke. Neither is it a precise statement of the diameter of the bore since certain tolerances are allowed; on balance it is best to think of the term as one which is descriptive but has lost its precise meaning. Guns smaller than 32-bore are described by stating the diameter of the barrel in decimal parts of an inch. The most common is the ·410, which is always so written but is spoken of as a 'four ten'.

Boxlock (or Box-lock)

A simple and effective form of lock, cheaper to make than the more complex sidelock.

Bring in

Beaters are said to bring in an area as they go through it beating out the game.

Brown

To shoot into the thick of a number of birds without selecting one as a target.

Butt (1)

A man-made place of concealment in which a gun may await the approach of driven grouse. Loosely applied to the screens sometimes used to conceal guns from driven partridges.

Butt (2)

Properly only the part of the stock of a shotgun which touches the shoulder when a gun is mounted; the upper part of the butt is called the heel, or the bump, while the lower part is called the toe. But the term is loosely used as an alternative to stock.

Cartridge extractor

A small tool with three claws which can be slipped over the rim on the base of a cartridge thus grasping it and enabling the user to pull a swollen case from the chamber of a gun.

Cast-off

The stock of a gun has cast-off if it is bent to the right of the line of the top rib to align the barrels with the vision of the shooter.

Cast-on

If the stock is bent to the left of the line of the barrels it is said to have cast-on.

Chamber

The portion of the bore of the barrel which has been enlarged to receive a cartridge. It is folly to use cartridges longer than those for which a gun is chambered although they may enter the chamber readily; but it is not dangerous to use shorter cartridges.

Chamber cone

The tapered portion of the bore joining the chamber to the true bore of the barrel.

Choke

Usually a slight constriction of the bore near the muzzle designed to concentrate the pellets; but something of the same effect can be obtained by enlarging the bore for a short distance and then reverting to the true bore. Chokes can be of varying degrees and their adjustment is an art rather than an exact science. A constriction of so many thousandths of an inch does not always result in the same concentration of the pattern and the layman is wise to specify the percentage of the pellets he wishes to strike within the prescribed circle and to leave the rest to the craftsmen who will regulate the choke.

Comb

Strictly only the part of the stock rising at an angle behind the grip should be called the comb but the name is often given to the whole of the top of the stock from the comb proper to the heel of the butt.

Covert

A wood. Pronounced 'cover'.

Covey

A group of partridges or grouse of a size to be expected from one brood.

Drive

One manœuvre by the beaters during which they bring in a certain area attempting to drive

	game to the shooters. Several drives make up one day's shooting at driven game.
Ejector gun	A shotgun which, when opened, throws out fired cartridges automatically. Such cartridges must be removed by hand from a non-ejector.
Extractor	The part of a gun which slides a short distance to the rear when the gun is opened, drawing the cartridge with it.
Flighting	The morning and evening flight of wildfowl to and from their feeding places; or the act of shooting wildfowl while so flying.
Flush	Game is said to flush when it flies up or breaks cover.
Flushing point	The place from which driven game may be expected to flush, often bushes specially planted in a covert.
Fore-end	The small part of a shotgun which clips onto the loop below the barrels.
Game licence	It is illegal to shoot any of the following birds without a game licence, which may be obtained at a Post Office: blackgame, capercailzie, grouse, pheasants, partridges, ptarmigan, snipe and woodcock. Notice that wildfowl are not included but that it is illegal to shoot them at certain times of the year. See *Game shooting season*.
Game shooting season	The period during which game may be shot legally. It is:

Grouse and ptarmigan, August 12th to December 10th.

Snipe, August 12th to January 31st.

Blackgame, August 20th to December 10th.

Wildfowl and woodcock in Scotland, September 1st to February 1st. But wildfowl in or above areas below the level of high water at ordinary spring tides may be shot from September 1st to February 20th.

Partridges, September 1st to February 1st.

Capercailzie and woodcock in England,

October 1st to January 31st.

Pheasants, October 1st to February 1st.

Rabbits and hares may be shot throughout the year.

In England and Wales it is illegal to shoot game on any Sunday or on Christmas Day.

In Scotland it is illegal to shoot any wild bird or animal on a Sunday or on Christmas Day.

Grip   See *hand*.

Hand   The thin part of the stock of a gun grasped by the trigger hand. Also called the grip, small of the stock or small of the butt.

Hide   A man-made place of concealment used by a shooter.

Jag   A brass fitting, around which rag or tow is wrapped, screwed to the end of a cleaning rod.

Loader   A man who loads a second gun for a shooter to fire.

Lock   In a shotgun it is the mechanism which fires the cartridge, so called, it is said, because this part was made by a locksmith in the old days.

Mount   To bring a gun to the shoulder, to take up the position from which the gun will be fired.

Mount 'on'   To mount 'on' a target is quite different from aiming. During aiming the shooter consciously looks at the sights and at the target, brings them all into focus and aligns them; but this should never be done while swinging a shotgun. In mounting 'on' the eyes are focused on the target and the barrels and muzzle are seen only hazily on the edge of conscious vision. In very quick shooting the muzzle may not be seen at all but one is usually conscious of its position much as one knows the whereabouts of the front of the car one is driving.

Pattern   The distribution of the pellets when a cartridge is fired. Patterns are compared by firing at a whitewashed iron plate (hence 'plating a gun') from a range of 40 yards and counting the pellets which strike within a circle whose diameter is 30 inches.

Poacher's pocket   A large pocket inside the lining of a shooting coat.

Poke   To aim a shotgun or to give the impression of doing so by waving the muzzle erratically instead of swinging it smoothly.

Proof marks   The marks stamped on barrels by the Proof House as a record of proving, usually found on the flats of the barrels.

Pump gun   A repeating shotgun actuated by sliding the fore-end back to eject a fired cartridge and forward to carry a live round from magazine to chamber.

Right and left   It is not enough to kill a bird with each barrel in rapid succession; this must be done but the intention to do so must be formed before the gun is mounted in the first instance.

Rough shoot   A shoot which derives little or no benefit from a gamekeeper.

Runner   A bird so wounded that it is able to run but cannot fly.

Sewelling   Also called *sewell* or *sewin*. A long string to which rags have been tied, used to flush driven pheasants or to serve as a stop.

Sidelock (or side-lock)   A type of lock which is mounted on plates at the sides of the action of a gun. Although more complex and hence more expensive than boxlocks, they were developed before boxlocks were invented. Sidelocks are more highly regarded but it is possible that boxlocks have overcome their late start and are now of equal merit.

Snap caps   Dummy cartridges. The strikers of a shotgun will be damaged if the triggers are pressed when the chambers are empty, so snap caps are loaded into the gun whenever one wishes to press the triggers without firing.

Stock   The wooden part of a shotgun behind the action.

Stop	Anything intended to prevent game running past a certain place or to make it fly. Stops range from a scrap of paper to a man with a gun.
Towered bird	A wounded bird which flies very steeply upward before falling. They are always stone dead on reaching the ground.
Try-gun	Essentially an ordinary gun whose stock can be adjusted, used by gunmakers when fitting guns.
Walk up (or walk-up)	Guns walking to rouse game which they will then shoot.

Index

171